FORWARD/COMMENTARY

The National Institute of Standards and Technology (NIST) is a measurement standards laboratory, and a non-regulatory agency of the United States Department of Commerce. Its mission is to promote innovation and industrial competitiveness. Founded in 1901, as the National Bureau of Standards, NIST was formed with the mandate to provide standard weights and measures, and to serve as the national physical laboratory for the United States. With a world-class measurement and testing laboratory encompassing a wide range of areas of computer science, mathematics, statistics, and systems engineering, NIST's cybersecurity program supports its overall mission to promote U.S. innovation and industrial competitiveness by advancing measurement science, standards, and related technology through research and development in ways that enhance economic security and improve our quality of life.

The need for cybersecurity standards and best practices that address interoperability, usability and privacy has been shown to be critical for the nation. NIST's cybersecurity programs seek to enable greater development and application of practical, innovative security technologies and methodologies that enhance the country's ability to address current and future computer and information security challenges.

The cybersecurity publications produced by NIST cover a wide range of cybersecurity concepts that are carefully designed to work together to produce a holistic approach to cybersecurity primarily for government agencies and constitute the best practices used by industry. This holistic strategy to cybersecurity covers the gamut of security subjects from development of secure encryption standards for communication and storage of information while at rest to how best to recover from a cyber-attack.

Why buy a book you can download for free?   **We print this so you don't have to.**

Some are available only in electronic media. Some online docs are missing pages or barely legible.

We at 4th Watch Publishing are former government employees, so we know how government employees actually use the standards. When a new standard is released, an engineer prints it out, punches holes and puts it in a 3-ring binder. While this is not a big deal for a 5 or 10-page document, many NIST documents are over 100 pages and printing a large document is a time-consuming effort. So, an engineer that's paid $75 an hour is spending hours simply printing out the tools needed to do the job. That's time that could be better spent doing engineering. We publish these documents so engineers can focus on what they were hired to do – engineering. It's much more cost-effective to just order the latest version from Amazon.com

If there is a standard you would like published, let us know. Our web site is usgovpub.com

Many of our titles are available as eBooks for Kindle, iPad, Nook, remarkable, BOOX, and Sony eReaders. Buy the paperback from Amazon and get Kindle eBook FREE using MATCHBOOK. Go to https://usgovpub.com to learn more.

Why buy an eBook when you can access data on a website for free? HYPERLINKS

Yes, many books are available as a PDF, but not all PDFs are bookmarked? Do you really want to search a 6,500-page PDF document manually? Load our copy onto your Kindle, PC, iPad, Android Tablet, Nook, or iPhone (download the FREE kindle App from the APP Store) and you have an easily searchable copy. Most devices will allow you to easily navigate an ePub to any Chapter. Note that there is a distinction between a Table of Contents and "Page Navigation". Page Navigation refers to a different sort of Table of Contents. Not one appearing as a page in the book, but one that shows up on the device itself when the reader accesses the navigation feature. Readers can click on a navigation link to jump to a Chapter or Subchapter. Once there, most devices allow you to "pinch and zoom" in or out to easily read the text. (Unfortunately, downloading the free sample file at Amazon.com does not include this feature. You have to buy a copy to get that functionality, but as inexpensive as eBooks are, it's worth it.) Kindle allows you to do word search and Page Flip (temporary place holder takes you back when you want to go back and check something). Visit **USGOVPUB.COM** to learn more.

**NIST Special Publication 800-56B
Revision 2**

Recommendation for Pair-Wise Key Establishment Using Integer Factorization Cryptography

Elaine Barker
Lily Chen
Allen Roginsky
Apostol Vassilev
Richard Davis
Scott Simon

This publication is available free of charge from:
https://doi.org/10.6028/NIST.SP.800-56Br2

COMPUTER SECURITY

National Institute of
Standards and Technology
U.S. Department of Commerce

NIST Special Publication 800-56B
Revision 2

Recommendation for Pair-Wise Key Establishment Using Integer Factorization Cryptography

Elaine Barker
Lily Chen
Allen Roginsky
Apostol Vassilev
Computer Security Division
Information Technology Laboratory

Richard Davis
Scott Simon
National Security Agency

March 2019

U.S. Department of Commerce
Wilbur L. Ross, Jr., Secretary

National Institute of Standards and Technology
Walter Copan, NIST Director and Under Secretary of Commerce for Standards and Technology

Authority

This publication has been developed by NIST in accordance with its statutory responsibilities under the Federal Information Security Modernization Act (FISMA) of 2014, 44 U.S.C. § 3551 *et seq.*, Public Law (P.L.) 113-283. NIST is responsible for developing information security standards and guidelines, including minimum requirements for federal information systems, but such standards and guidelines shall not apply to national security systems without the express approval of appropriate federal officials exercising policy authority over such systems. This guideline is consistent with the requirements of the Office of Management and Budget (OMB) Circular A-130.

Nothing in this publication should be taken to contradict the standards and guidelines made mandatory and binding on federal agencies by the Secretary of Commerce under statutory authority. Nor should these guidelines be interpreted as altering or superseding the existing authorities of the Secretary of Commerce, Director of the OMB, or any other federal official. This publication may be used by nongovernmental organizations on a voluntary basis and is not subject to copyright in the United States. Attribution would, however, be appreciated by NIST.

National Institute of Standards and Technology Special Publication 800-56B Revision 2
Natl. Inst. Stand. Technol. Spec. Publ. 800-56B Rev. 2, 131 pages (March 2019)
CODEN: NSPUE2

This publication is available free of charge from:
https://doi.org/10.6028/NIST.SP.800-56Br2

Comments on this publication may be submitted to:

National Institute of Standards and Technology
Attn: Computer Security Division, Information Technology Laboratory
100 Bureau Drive (Mail Stop 8930) Gaithersburg, MD 20899-8930
Email: SP800-56b_comments@nist.gov

All comments are subject to release under the Freedom of Information Act (FOIA).

Reports on Computer Systems Technology

The Information Technology Laboratory (ITL) at the National Institute of Standards and Technology (NIST) promotes the U.S. economy and public welfare by providing technical leadership for the Nation's measurement and standards infrastructure. ITL develops tests, test methods, reference data, proof of concept implementations, and technical analyses to advance the development and productive use of information technology. ITL's responsibilities include the development of management, administrative, technical, and physical standards and guidelines for the cost-effective security and privacy of other than national security-related information in Federal information systems. The Special Publication 800-series reports on ITL's research, guidelines, and outreach efforts in information system security, and its collaborative activities with industry, government, and academic organizations.

Abstract

This Recommendation specifies key-establishment schemes using integer factorization cryptography (in particular, RSA). Both key-agreement and key transport schemes are specified for pairs of entities, and methods for key confirmation are included to provide assurance that both parties share the same keying material. In addition, the security properties associated with each scheme are provided.

Keywords

assurances; integer factorization cryptography; key agreement; key confirmation; key derivation; key establishment; key management; key recovery; key transport.

Acknowledgements

NIST thanks the many contributions by the public and private sectors whose thoughtful and constructive comments improved the quality and usefulness of this publication. The authors also acknowledge the contributions by Dustin Moody, Andrew Regenscheid and Miles Smid made to previous versions of this Recommendation.

Conformance Testing

Conformance testing for implementations of this Recommendation will be conducted within the framework of the Cryptographic Algorithm Validation Program (CAVP) and the Cryptographic Module Validation Program (CMVP). The requirements of this Recommendation are indicated by the word "**shall**." Some of these requirements may be out-of-scope for CAVP or CMVP validation testing, and thus are the responsibility of entities using, implementing, installing or configuring applications that incorporate this Recommendation.

Table of Contents

Figures

Tables

1. Introduction

Many U.S. Government Information Technology (IT) systems need to employ strong cryptographic schemes to protect the integrity and confidentiality of the data that they process. Algorithms such as the Advanced Encryption Standard (AES), as defined in Federal Information Processing Standard (FIPS) 197,[1] and HMAC, as defined in FIPS 198,[2] make attractive choices for the provision of these services. These algorithms have been standardized to facilitate interoperability between systems. However, the use of these algorithms requires the establishment of secret keying material that is shared in advance. Trusted couriers may manually distribute this secret keying material, but as the number of entities using a system grows, the work involved in the distribution of the secret keying material grows rapidly. Therefore, it is essential to support the cryptographic algorithms used in modern U.S. Government applications with automated key-establishment schemes.

This Recommendation provides the specifications of key-establishment schemes that are appropriate for use by the U.S. Federal Government, based on a standard that was developed by the Accredited Standards Committee (ASC) X9, Inc: ANS X9.44.[3] A key-establishment scheme can be characterized as either a key-agreement scheme or a key-transport scheme. This Recommendation provides key-agreement and key-transport schemes that are based on the Rivest Shamir Adleman (RSA) asymmetric-key algorithm.

2. Scope and Purpose

This Recommendation is intended for use in conjunction with NIST Special Publication (SP) 800-57.[4] This key-establishment Recommendation, SP 800-57, and FIPS 186[5] are intended to provide information for a vendor to implement secure key-establishment using asymmetric algorithms in FIPS 140[6] validated modules.

Note that a key-establishment scheme is a component of a protocol that may provide security properties not provided by the scheme when considered by itself; protocols, per se, are not specified in this Recommendation.

---

[1] FIPS 197, *Advanced Encryption Standard (AES)*.

[2] FIPS 198, *Keyed-hash Message Authentication Code (HMAC)*.

[3] ANS X9.44, *Key Establishment using Integer Factorization Cryptography*.

[4] SP 800-57, *Recommendation for Key Management, Part 1: General*.

[5] FIPS 186, *Digital Signature Standard (DSS)*.

[6] FIPS 140, *Security Requirements for Cryptographic Modules*.

3. Definitions, Symbols and Abbreviations

3.1   Definitions

Additional input	Information known by two parties that is cryptographically bound to the secret keying material being protected using the encryption operation.
Algorithm	A clearly specified mathematical process for computation; a set of rules that, if followed, will give a prescribed result.
Approved	FIPS-**approved** or NIST-Recommended. An algorithm or technique that is either 1) specified in a FIPS or NIST Recommendation, or 2) adopted in a FIPS or NIST Recommendation and specified either (a) in an appendix to the FIPS or NIST Recommendation, or (b) in a document referenced by the FIPS or NIST Recommendation.
Assumption	Used to indicate the conditions that are required to be true when an **approved** key-establishment scheme is executed in accordance with this Recommendation.
Assurance of private key possession	Confidence that an entity possesses a private key associated with a given public key.
Assurance of validity	Confidence that an RSA key pair is arithmetically correct.
Big-endian	The property of a byte string having its bytes positioned in order of decreasing significance. In particular, the leftmost (first) byte is the most significant byte (containing the most significant eight bits of the corresponding bit string) and the rightmost (last) byte is the least significant byte (containing the least significant eight bits of the corresponding bit string). For the purposes of this Recommendation, it is assumed that the bits within each byte of a big-endian byte string are also positioned in order of decreasing significance (beginning with the most significant bit in the leftmost position and ending with the least significant bit in the rightmost position).
Binding	Assurance of the integrity of an asserted relationship between items of information that is provided by cryptographic means. Also see Trusted association.
Bit length	A positive integer that expresses the number of bits in a bit string.
Bit string	An ordered sequence of 0's and 1's. Also known as a binary string.

Byte	A bit string consisting of eight bits.
Byte length	A positive integer that expresses the number of bytes in a byte string.
Byte string	An ordered sequence of bytes.
Certificate Authority (CA)	The entity in a Public Key Infrastructure (PKI) that is responsible for issuing public-key certificates and exacting compliance to a PKI policy. Also known as a Certification Authority.
Ciphertext	Data in its enciphered form.
Confidentiality	The property that sensitive information is not disclosed to unauthorized entities.
Critical security parameter (CSP)	Security-related information whose disclosure or modification can compromise the security of a cryptographic module. Domain parameters, secret or private keys, shared secrets, key-derivation keys, intermediate values and secret salts are examples of quantities that may be considered critical security parameters in this Recommendation. See FIPS 140.
Cryptographic key (Key)	A parameter used with a cryptographic algorithm that determines its operation.
Decryption	The process of transforming ciphertext into plaintext using a cryptographic algorithm and key.
Destroy	In this Recommendation, an action applied to a key or a piece of secret data. After a key or a piece of secret data is destroyed, no information about its value can be recovered. Also known as *zeroization* in FIPS 140.
Encryption	The process of transforming plaintext into ciphertext using a cryptographic algorithm and key.
Entity	An individual (person), organization, device, or process. "Party" is a synonym.
Fresh	Newly established secret keying material that is statistically independent of any previously established keying material.
Greatest common divisor	The largest positive integer that divides each of two or more positive integers without a remainder.

Hash function	A function that maps a bit string of arbitrary length to a fixed-length bit string. **Approved** hash functions are expected to satisfy the following properties: 1. One-way: It is computationally infeasible to find any input that maps to any pre-specified output, and 2. Collision resistant: It is computationally infeasible to find any two distinct inputs that map to the same output.
Hash value	The fixed-length bit string produced by a hash function.
Identifier	A bit string that is associated with a person, device or organization. It may be an identifying name, or may be something more abstract (for example, a string consisting of an Internet Protocol (IP) address).
Integrity	A property whereby data has not been altered in an unauthorized manner since it was created, transmitted or stored.
Key agreement	A (pair-wise) key-establishment procedure where the resultant secret keying material is a function of information contributed by two participants so that no party can predetermine the value of the secret keying material independently from the contributions of the other party. Contrast with key-transport.
Key-agreement transaction	An execution of a key-agreement scheme.
Key confirmation	A procedure to provide assurance to one party (the key-confirmation recipient) that another party (the key-confirmation provider) possesses the correct secret keying material and/or shared secret from which that secret keying material is derived.
Key-confirmation provider	The party that provides assurance to the other party (the recipient) that the two parties have indeed established a shared secret or shared keying material.
Key-derivation function	As used in this Recommendation, a function used to derive secret keying material from a shared secret (or a key) and other information.
Key-derivation method	As used in this Recommendation, a method by which secret keying material is derived from a shared secret and other information. A key-derivation method may use a key-derivation function or a key-derivation procedure.

Key-derivation procedure	As used in this Recommendation, a multi-step process to derive secret keying material from a shared secret and other information.
Key establishment	A procedure that results in establishing secret keying material that is shared among different parties.
Key-establishment key pair	A private/public key pair used in a key-establishment scheme.
Key-establishment transaction	An instance of establishing secret keying material using a key-agreement or key-transport transaction.
Key pair	See key-establishment key pair.
Key transport	A (pair-wise) key-establishment procedure whereby one party (the sender) selects a value for the secret keying material and then securely distributes that value to another party (the receiver). Contrast with key agreement.
Key-transport transaction	An execution of a key-transport scheme.
Key wrapping	A method of protecting secret keying material (along with associated integrity information) that provides both confidentiality and integrity protection when using symmetric-key algorithms.
Key-wrapping key	A symmetric key used with a key-wrapping algorithm to protect keying material. In accordance with this Recommendation (SP 800-56B), a key-wrapping key can be established using a **KAS1**, **KAS2** or **KTS-OAEP** scheme and then used with a key-wrapping algorithm to protect transported keying material. (See Section 9.3.)
Keying material	Data that is represented as a binary string such that any non-overlapping segments of the string with the required lengths can be used as secret keys, secret initialization vectors and other secret parameters.
Least common multiple	The smallest positive integer that is divisible by two or more positive integers without a remainder. For example, the least common multiple of 2 and 3 is 6.
MAC tag	Data obtained from the output of a MAC algorithm (possibly by truncation) that can be used by an entity to verify the integrity and the origination of the information used as input to the MAC algorithm.

Message Authentication Code (MAC) algorithm	A family of cryptographic functions that is parameterized by a symmetric key. Each of the functions can act on input data (called a "message") of variable length to produce an output value of a specified length. The output value is called the MAC of the input message. An **approved** MAC algorithm is expected to satisfy the following property (for each of its supported security levels):
	It must be computationally infeasible to determine the (as yet unseen) MAC of a message without knowledge of the key, even if one has already seen the results of using that key to compute the MACs of other (different) messages.
	A MAC algorithm can be used to provide data-origin authentication and data-integrity protection. In this Recommendation, a MAC algorithm is used for key confirmation; the use of MAC algorithms for key derivation is addressed in SP 800-56C.[7]
Nonce	A time-varying value that has an acceptably small chance of repeating. For example, a nonce is a random value that is generated anew for each use, a timestamp, a sequence number, or some combination of these.
Owner	For a key pair, the owner is the entity that is authorized to use the private key associated with a public key, whether that entity generated the key pair itself or a trusted party generated the key pair for the entity.
Party	See entity.
Prime number	An integer greater than 1 that has no positive integer factors other than 1 and itself.
Primitive	A low-level cryptographic algorithm that is used as a basic building block for higher-level cryptographic operations or schemes.
Private key	A cryptographic key that is kept secret and is used with a public-key cryptographic algorithm. A private key is associated with a public key.
Protocol	A set of rules used by two or more communicating entities that describe the message order and data structures for information exchanged between the entities.

---

[7] SP 800-56C, *Recommendation for Key-Derivation Methods in Key-Establishment Schemes.*

Provider	A party that provides (1) a public key (e.g., in a certificate); (2) assurance, such as an assurance of the validity of a candidate public key or assurance of possession of the private key associated with a public key; or (3) key confirmation. Contrast with recipient.
Public key	A cryptographic key that may be made public and is used with a public-key cryptographic algorithm. A public key is associated with a private key.
Public-key algorithm	A cryptographic algorithm that uses two related keys: a public key and a private key. The two keys have the property that determining the private key from the public key is computationally infeasible.
Public-key certificate	A data structure that contains an entity's identifier(s), the entity's public key (including an indication of the associated set of domain parameters) and possibly other information, along with a signature on that data set that is generated by a trusted party, i.e., a certificate authority, thereby binding the public key to the included identifier(s).
Public-key cryptography	A form of cryptography that uses two related keys, a public key and a private key; the two keys have the property that, given the public key, it is computationally infeasible to derive the private key. For key establishment, public-key cryptography allows different parties to communicate securely without having prior access to a secret key that is shared, by using one or more pairs (public key and private key) of cryptographic keys.
Public-key validation	The procedure whereby the recipient of a public key checks that the key conforms to the arithmetic requirements for such a key in order to thwart certain types of attacks.
Random nonce	A nonce containing a random-value component that is generated anew for each nonce.
Receiver	The party that receives secret keying material via a key-transport transaction. Contrast with sender.
Recipient	A party that either (1) receives a public key; or (2) obtains assurance from an assurance provider (e.g., assurance of the validity of a candidate public key or assurance of possession of the private key corresponding to a public key); or (3) receives key confirmation from a key-confirmation provider.

Relatively prime	Two positive integers are relatively prime if their greatest common divisor is 1.
Scheme	A set of unambiguously specified transformations that provide a (cryptographic) service when properly implemented and maintained. A scheme is a higher-level construct than a primitive and a lower-level construct than a protocol.
Security properties	The security features (e.g., replay protection, or key confirmation) that a cryptographic scheme may, or may not, provide.
Security strength (also, "Bits of security")	A number associated with the amount of work (that is, the number of operations) that is required to break a cryptographic algorithm or system.
Sender	The party that sends secret keying material to the receiver using a key-transport transaction. Contrast with receiver.
Shall	This term is used to indicate a requirement that needs to be fulfilled to claim conformance to this Recommendation. Note that **shall** may be coupled with **not** to become **shall not**.
Shared secret	A secret value that has been computed during the execution of a key-establishment scheme, is known by both participants, and is used as input to a key-derivation method to produce secret keying material.
Should	This term is used to indicate an important recommendation. Ignoring the recommendation could result in undesirable results. Note that **should** may be coupled with **not** to become **should not**.
Support (a security strength)	A security strength of s bits is said to be supported by a particular choice of algorithm, primitive, auxiliary function, parameters (etc.) for use in the implementation of a cryptographic mechanism if that choice will not prevent the resulting implementation from attaining a security strength of at least s bits. In this Recommendation, it is assumed that implementation choices are intended to support a security strength of 112 bits or more (see [SP 800-57][8] and [SP 800-131A][9]).

---

[8] SP 800-57 Rev. 4, *Recommendation for Key Management Part1: General.*

[9] SP 800-131A, *Transitions: Recommendation for Transitioning the Use of Cryptographic Algorithms and Key Lengths.*

Symmetric key	A cryptographic key that is shared between two or more entities and used with a cryptographic application to process information.
Symmetric-key algorithm	A cryptographic algorithm that uses secret keying material that is shared between authorized parties.
Targeted security strength	The security strength that is intended to be supported by one or more implementation-related choices (such as algorithms, primitives, auxiliary functions, parameter sizes and/or actual parameters) for the purpose of instantiating a cryptographic mechanism. In this Recommendation, it is assumed that the targeted security strength of any instantiation of an **approved** key-establishment scheme has a value greater than or equal to 112 bits and less than or equal to 256 bits.
Trusted association	Assurance of the integrity of an asserted relationship between items of information that may be provided by cryptographic or non-cryptographic (e.g., physical) means. Also see Binding.
Trusted party	A party that is trusted by an entity to faithfully perform certain services for that entity. An entity may choose to act as a trusted party for itself.
Trusted third party	A third party, such as a CA, that is trusted by its clients to perform certain services. (By contrast, the two participants in a key-establishment transaction are considered to be the first and second parties.)

3.2   Symbols and Abbreviations

A	Additional input that is bound to the secret keying material; a byte string.
$[a, b]$	The set of integers x such that $a \leq x \leq b$.
AES	Advanced Encryption Standard (as specified in FIPS 197).
ANS	American National Standard.
ASC	The Accredited Standards Committee of the American National Standards Institute (ANSI).
ASN.1	Abstract Syntax Notation One.

BS2I	Byte String to Integer conversion routine.
c	Ciphertext (expressed as an integer).
C, C_U, C_V	Ciphertext (expressed as a byte string).
CA	Certification Authority.
CRT	Chinese Remainder Theorem.
d	RSA private exponent; a positive integer.
Data	A variable-length string of zero or more (eight-bit) bytes.
DerivedKeyingMaterial	Derived keying material; a bit string.
dP	RSA private exponent for the prime factor p in the CRT format, i.e., $d \bmod (p-1)$; an integer.
dQ	RSA private exponent for the prime factor q in the CRT format, i.e., $d \bmod (q-1)$; an integer.
e	RSA public exponent; a positive integer.
eBits	The bit length of the RSA exponent e.
ES(*nBits*)	The estimated maximum security strength for an RSA modulus of length *nBits* (see <u>Table 2</u>).
GCD(a, b)	Greatest Common Divisor of two positive integers a and b. For example, GCD(12, 16) = 4.
HMAC	Keyed-hash Message Authentication Code (as specified in <u>FIPS 198)</u>.
HMAC-*hash*	Keyed-hash Message Authentication Code (as specified in FIPS 198) with an **approved** hash function *hash*.
I2BS	Integer to Byte String conversion routine.
ID	The bit string denoting the identifier associated with an entity.
ID_P, ID_R, ID_U, ID_V	Identifier bit strings for parties P, R, U, and V, respectively.
IFC	Integer Factorization Cryptography.

K	Keying material; a byte string.
KBits	The bit length of the secret keying material.
KAS	Key-Agreement Scheme.
KAS1-basic	The basic form of Key-Agreement Scheme 1.
KAS1-Party_V-confirmation	Key-Agreement Scheme 1 with confirmation by party V. Previously known as KAS1-responder-confirmation.
KAS2-basic	The basic form of Key-Agreement Scheme 2.
KAS2-bilateral-confirmation	Key-Agreement Scheme 2 with bilateral confirmation.
KAS2-Party_V-confirmation	Key-Agreement Scheme 2 with confirmation by party V. Previously known as KAS2-responder-confirmation.
KAS2-Party_U-confirmation	Key-Agreement Scheme 2 with confirmation by party U. Previously known as KAS2-initiator-confirmation.
KC	Key Confirmation.
KDM	Key-Derivation Method.
KeyData	Keying material other than that which is used for the *MacKey* employed in key confirmation.
KTS	Key-transport Scheme.
KTS-OAEP-basic	The basic form of the key-transport Scheme with Optimal Asymmetric Encryption Padding.
KTS-OAEP-Party_V-confirmation	Key-transport Scheme with Optimal Asymmetric Encryption Padding and key confirmation provided by party V. Previously known as KTS-OAEP-receiver-confirmation.
LCM(a, b)	Least Common Multiple of two positive integers a and b. For example, LCM(4, 6) = 12.
len(x)	For the non-negative integer x, the bit length of the shortest bit string that can be interpreted as a binary (i.e., base two) representation of the integer x. For integer $x > 0$, len(x) = $\lfloor \log_2(x) \rfloor + 1$. (In the case of 0, len(0) = 1.)

MAC	Message Authentication Code.
MacData	A byte string input to the *MacTag* computation.
MacData$_U$, (or MacData$_V$)	*MacData* associated with party U (or party V, respectively), and used to generate *MacTag$_U$ (or MacTag$_V$,* respectively*)*. Each is a byte string.
MacKey	Key used to compute the MAC; a byte string.
MacKeyBits	The bit length of *MacKey* such that *MacKeyBits* = 8 × *MacKeyLen.*
MacKeyLen	The byte length of the *MacKey.*
MacOutputBits	The bit length of the MAC output block such that *MacOutputBits* = 8 × *MacOutputLen.*
MacOutputLen	The byte length of the MAC output block.
MacTag	A byte string that allows an entity to verify the integrity of the information. *MacTag* is the output from the MAC algorithm (possibly after truncation). The literature sometimes refers to *MacTag* as a Message Authentication Code (MAC).
MacTag$_V$, (MacTag$_U$)	The *MacTag* generated by party V (or party U, respectively). Each is a byte string.
MacTagBits	The bit length of the MAC tag such that *MacTagBits* = 8 × *MacTagLen.*
MacTagLen	The byte length of *MacTag.*
Mask	Mask; a byte string.
MGF	Mask Generation Function.
mgfSeed	String from which a mask is derived; a byte string.
n	RSA modulus. $n = pq$, where p and q are distinct odd primes.
(n, d)	RSA private key in the basic format.
(n, e)	RSA public key.

$(n, e, d, p, q, dP, dQ, qInv)$	RSA private key in the Chinese Remainder Theorem (CRT) format.
N_V	Nonce contributed by party V; a byte string.
nBits	The bit length of the RSA modulus n.
nLen	The byte length of the RSA modulus n. (Note that in FIPS 186, nlen refers to the bit length of n.)
Null	The empty bit string.
OtherInput	Other information for key derivation; a bit string.
p	First prime factor of the RSA modulus n.
(p, q, d)	RSA private key in the prime-factor format.
$PrivKey_U$, $PrivKey_V$	Private key of party U or V, respectively.
$PubKey_U$, $PubKey_V$	Public key of party U or V, respectively.
q	Second prime factor of the RSA modulus n.
qInv	Inverse of q modulo p in the CRT format, i.e., $q^{-1} \bmod p$; an integer.
RBG	Random Bit Generator.
RSA	Rivest-Shamir-Adleman algorithm
RSASVE	RSA Secret Value Encapsulation.
RSA-OAEP	RSA with Optimal Asymmetric Encryption Padding.
S	String of bytes.
s	Security strength in bits.
SHA	Secure Hash Algorithm.

$T_{MacTagBits}(X)$	A truncation function that outputs the most significant (i.e., leftmost) *MacTagBits* bits of the input string, X, when the bit length of X is greater than *MacTagBits*; otherwise, the function outputs X. For example, $T_2(1011) = 10$, $T_3(1011) = 101$, and $T_4(1011) = 1011$.
TransportedKeyingMaterial	Transported keying material.
TTP	A Trusted Third Party.
U	One party in a key-establishment scheme.
V	Another party in a key-establishment scheme.
X	Byte string to be converted to or from an integer; the output of conversion from an ASCII string.
$X = ? \ Y$	Check for the equality of X and Y.
$x \bmod n$	The modular reduction of the (arbitrary) integer x by the positive integer n (the *modulus*). For the purposes of this Recommendation, $y = x \bmod n$ is the unique integer satisfying the following two conditions: 1) $0 \le y < n$, and 2) $x - y$ is divisible by n.
$x^{-1} \bmod n$	The multiplicative inverse of the integer x modulo the positive integer n. This quantity is defined if and only if x is relatively prime to n. For the purposes of this Recommendation, $y = x^{-1} \bmod n$ is the unique integer satisfying the following two conditions: 1) $0 \le y < n$, and 2) $1 = (xy) \bmod n$.
$\{X\}$	Indicates that the inclusion of X is optional.
$\{x, y\}$	A set containing the integers x and y.
$x \times y$ xy	The product of x and y.
$X \parallel Y$	Concatenation of two strings X and Y.
$\lceil x \rceil$	The ceiling of x; the smallest integer $\ge x$. For example, $\lceil 5 \rceil = 5$ and $\lceil 5.3 \rceil = 6$.

$\lfloor x \rfloor$	The floor of x; the greatest integer that does not exceed x. For example, $\lfloor 2.1 \rfloor = 2$, and $\lfloor 4 \rfloor = 4$.
$\lvert x \rvert$	The absolute value of x.
Z	A shared secret that is used to derive secret keying material using a key-derivation method; a byte string.
$\lambda(n)$	Lambda function of the RSA modulus n, i.e., the least positive integer i such that $1 = a^i \bmod n$ for all a relatively prime to n. When $n = p \times q$, $\lambda(n) = \mathrm{LCM}(p - 1, q - 1)$.
$\oplus$	Exclusive-Or (XOR) operation, defined as bit-wise modulo 2 arithmetic with no carry.

4   Key-Establishment Schemes Overview

Secret cryptographic keying material may be electronically established between parties by using a key-establishment scheme, that is, by using either a key-agreement scheme or a key-transport scheme. Key-establishment schemes may use either symmetric-key techniques or asymmetric-key techniques or both. The key-establishment schemes described in this Recommendation use asymmetric-key techniques.

In this Recommendation, the **approved** key-establishment schemes are described in terms of the roles played by parties "U" and "V." These are specific labels that are used to distinguish between the two participants engaged in key establishment – irrespective of the actual labels that may be used by a protocol employing a particular **approved** key-establishment scheme.

During key agreement, the derived secret keying material is the result of contributions made by both parties. To be in conformance with this Recommendation, a protocol employing any of the **approved** pair-wise key-agreement schemes **shall** unambiguously assign the roles of U and V to the participants by clearly defining which participant performs the actions ascribed by this Recommendation to party U, and which performs the actions ascribed herein to party V.

During key transport, one party selects the secret keying material to be transported. The secret keying material is then encrypted using RSA, and sent to the other party. The party that sends the secret keying material is called the sender, and the other party is called the receiver.

The security of the Integer Factorization Cryptography (IFC) schemes in this Recommendation relies on the intractability of factoring integers that are products of two sufficiently large, distinct prime numbers. All IFC schemes in this Recommendation are based on RSA.

The security of an IFC scheme also depends on its implementation, and this document includes a number of practical recommendations for implementers. For example, good security practice dictates that implementations of procedures employed by primitives, operations, schemes, etc., include steps that destroy any potentially sensitive locally stored data that is created (and/or copied for use) during the execution of a particular procedure, and whose continued local storage is not required after the procedure has been exited. The destruction of such locally stored data ideally occurs prior to or during any exit from the procedure. This is intended to limit opportunities for unauthorized access to sensitive information that might compromise a key-establishment process.

Explicit instructions for the destruction of certain potentially sensitive values that are likely to be locally stored by procedures are included in the specifications found in this Recommendation. Examples of such values include local copies of any portions of secret or private keys that are employed or generated during the execution of a procedure, intermediate results produced during computations, and locally stored duplicates of values that are ultimately output by a procedure. However, it is not possible to anticipate the form of all possible implementations of the specified primitives, operations, schemes, etc., making it impossible to enumerate all potentially sensitive data that might be locally stored by a procedure employed in a particular implementation. Nevertheless, the destruction of any potentially sensitive locally stored data is an obligation of all implementations.

Error handling can also be an issue. Section 7 cautions implementers to handle error messages in a manner that avoids revealing even partial information about the decryption/decoding processes that may be performed during the execution of a particular procedure.

For compliance with this Recommendation, equivalent processes may be used. Two processes are equivalent if, whenever the same values are input to each process (either as input parameters or as values made available during the process), each process produces the same output as the other.

Some processes are used to provide assurance (for example, assurance of the arithmetic validity of a public key or assurance of the possession of a private key associated with a public key). The party that provides the assurance is called the provider (of the assurance), and the other party is called the recipient (of the assurance).

Several steps are performed to establish secret keying material as described in Sections 4.1, 4.2, and 4.3.

4.1   Key-Establishment Preparations

The owner of a private/public key pair is the entity that is authorized to use the private key of that key pair. Figure 1 depicts the steps that may be required of that entity when preparing for a key-establishment process (i.e., either key agreement or key transport).

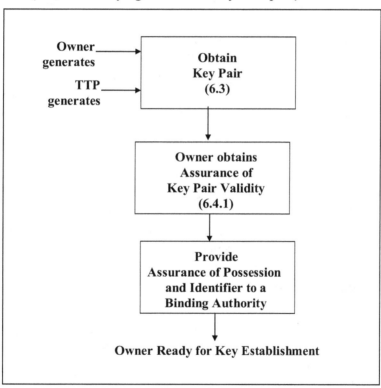

Figure 1: Owner Key-establishment Preparations

The first step in the preparation is for the entity to obtain a key pair. Either the entity (i.e., the owner) generates the key pair as specified in Section 6.3, or a trusted third party (TTP) generates the key pair as specified in Section 6.3 and provides it to the owner. If the key pair is generated by a trusted third party, then the key pair **shall** be transported to the owner in a protected manner (providing source authentication and integrity protection for the entire key pair, and confidentiality protection for (at least) the private key). The owner obtains assurance of key-pair validity and, as part of the process, obtains assurance that it actually possesses the (correct) private key. **Approved** methods for obtaining assurance of key-pair validity by the owner are provided in Section 6.4.1.

An identifier is used to label the entity that owns a key pair used in a key-establishment transaction. This label may uniquely distinguish the entity from all others, in which case it could rightfully be considered an identity. However, the label may be something less specific – an organization, nickname, etc. – hence, the term *identifier* is used in this Recommendation, rather than the term *identity*. For example, an identifier could be "NIST123," rather than an identifier that names a particular person. A key pair's owner (or an agent trusted to act on the owner's behalf) is responsible for ensuring that the identifier associated with its public key is appropriate for the applications in which the public key will be used.

For each key pair, this Recommendation assumes that there is a trusted association between the owner's identifier(s) and the owner's public key. The association may be provided using cryptographic mechanisms or by physical means. The use of cryptographic mechanisms may require the use of a binding authority (i.e., a trusted authority) that binds the information in a manner that can be verified by others; an example of such a trusted authority is a registration authority working with a CA who creates a certificate containing both the public key and the identifier(s). The binding authority **shall** verify the owner's intent to associate the public key with the specific identifier(s) chosen for the owner; the means for accomplishing this is beyond the scope of this Recommendation. The binding authority **shall** obtain assurance of both the arithmetic validity of the owner's public key and the owner's possession of the private key corresponding to that public key. (**Approved** techniques that can be employed by the binding authority to obtain these assurances are described in Section 6.4.2.1 [method 1], Section 6.4.2.2, Section 6.4.2.3 and Section 6.4.2.3.2.)

As an alternative to reliance upon a binding authority, trusted associations between identifiers and public keys may be established by the direct exchange of this information between entities, using a mutually trusted method (e.g., a trusted courier or a face-to-face exchange). In this case, each entity receiving a public key and associated identifier(s) **shall** be responsible for obtaining the same assurances that would have been obtained on the entity's behalf by a binding authority (see the previous paragraph). Entities **shall** also be responsible for maintaining (by cryptographic or other means) the trusted associations between any identifiers and public keys received through such exchanges.

If an entity engaged in a key-establishment transaction owns a key pair that is employed during the transaction, then the identifier used to label that party **shall** be one that has a trusted association with the public key of that key pair. If an entity engaged in a key-establishment transaction does not employ a key pair during the transaction, but an identifier is still desired/required for that party, then a non-null identifier **shall** be selected/assigned in accordance with the requirements of the protocol relying upon the transaction.

After the above steps have been performed, the key-pair owner is ready to enter into a key-establishment process.

4.2   Key-Agreement Process

Figure 2 depicts the steps implemented by an entity when establishing secret keying material with another entity using one of the key-agreement schemes described in Section 8 of this Recommendation. (Some discrepancies in ordering may occur in practice, depending on the communication protocol in which the key-agreement process is performed.) Depending on the key-agreement scheme, the party whose actions are described could be either of the two participants in the key-agreement scheme (i.e., either party U or party V). Note that some of the actions shown may not be a part of every scheme. For example, key confirmation is not provided in the basic key-agreement schemes (see Sections 8.2.2 and 8.3.2). The specifications of this Recommendation indicate when a particular action is required.

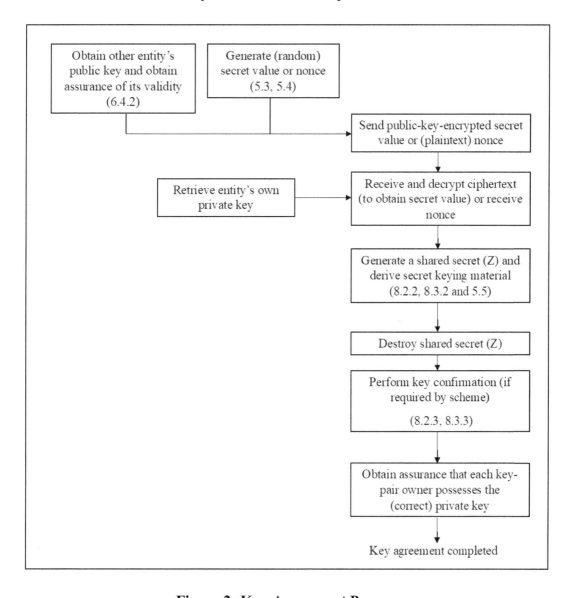

Figure 2: Key-Agreement Process

Each participant that is required to do so by the key-agreement scheme or the relying application/protocol obtains an identifier associated with the other entity, and verifies that the identifier of the other entity corresponds to the entity with whom the participant wishes to establish secret keying material.

Each entity that requires the other entity's public key for use in the key-agreement scheme obtains a public key that has a trusted association with the other party's identifier, and obtains assurance of the validity of the public key. **Approved** methods for obtaining assurance of the validity of another entity's public key are provided in Section 6.4.2.

Each entity generates either a (random) secret value or a nonce, as required by the particular key-agreement scheme. If the scheme requires an entity to generate a secret value, that secret value is generated as specified in Section 5.3 and encrypted using the other entity's public key. The resulting ciphertext is then provided to the other entity. If the key-agreement scheme requires that an entity provide a nonce, that nonce is generated as specified in Section 5.4 and provided (in plaintext form) to the other party. (See Sections 8.2 and 8.3 for details).

Each participant in the key-agreement process uses the appropriate public and/or private keys to establish a shared secret (Z) as specified in Section 8.2.2 or 8.3.2. Each participant then derives secret keying material from the shared secret (and other information), as specified in Section 5.5.

If the key-agreement scheme includes key confirmation provided by one or both of the participants, then key confirmation is performed as specified in Section 8.2.3 or 8.3.3. When performed in accordance with those sections, successful key confirmation may also provide assurance that a key-pair owner possesses the (correct) private key (see Section 6.4.2.3.2).

The owner of any key pair used during the key-agreement transaction is required to have assurance that the owner is in possession of the correct private key. Likewise, the recipient of another entity's public key is required to have assurance that its owner is in possession of the corresponding private key. Assurance of private-key possession is obtained prior to using the derived keying material for purposes beyond those of the key-agreement transaction itself. This assurance may be provided/obtained either through key confirmation, or by some other **approved** means (see Sections 6.4.1 and 6.4.2).

4.3   Key-Transport Process

Figure 3 depicts the steps implemented by two entities when using the key-transport schemes described in Section 9.2 of this Recommendation to establish secret keying material.

The entity who will act as the sender obtains the identifier associated with the entity that will act as the receiver, and verifies that the receiver's identifier corresponds to an entity to whom the sender wishes to send secret keying material.

Prior to performing key transport, the sender obtains the receiver's public key and obtains assurance of its validity. **Approved** methods for obtaining assurance of the validity of another entity's public key are provided in Section 6.4.2. The sender is also required to have assurance that the receiver is in possession of the private key corresponding to the receiver's public key prior to key transport, unless that assurance is obtained via the key confirmation steps that are included as part of the scheme. (See Section 9.2 for details).

20

The sender selects the secret keying material (and, perhaps, additional input) to be transported to the other entity. Then, using the intended receiver's public key, the sender encrypts that material directly (see Section 9.2.3). The resulting ciphertext is transported to the receiver.

Prior to participating in a key-transport transaction, the receiver is required to have assurance of the validity of its own key pair. This assurance may be renewed whenever desired. Upon (or before) receipt of the transported ciphertext, the receiver retrieves the private key from its own key pair. Using its private key, the receiver takes the necessary steps (as specified in Section 9.2.3) to decrypt the ciphertext and obtain the transported plaintext keying material.

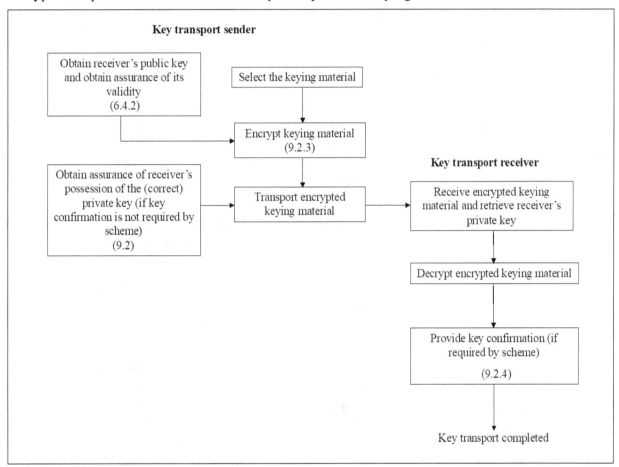

Figure 3: Key-Transport Process

If the key-transport scheme includes key confirmation, then key confirmation is provided by the receiver to the sender as specified in Section 9.2.4. Through the use of key confirmation, the sender can obtain assurance that the receiver has correctly recovered the keying material from the ciphertext. Successful key confirmation may also provide assurance that the receiver was in possession of the correct private key (see Section 6.4.2.3.2).

An additional method for key transport is discussed in Section 9.3.

5 Cryptographic Elements

This section describes the basic cryptographic elements that support the development of the key-establishment schemes specified in this Recommendation. The schemes described herein are based upon the correct implementation of these elements.

5.1 Cryptographic Hash Functions

In this Recommendation, cryptographic hash functions may be used for mask generation during RSA-OAEP encryption/decryption, in key derivation, and/or in MAC-tag computation during key confirmation. An **approved** hash function **shall** be used when a hash function is required (see FIPS 180[10] and FIPS 202[11]).

5.2 Message Authentication Code (MAC) Algorithms

A Message Authentication Code (MAC) algorithm defines a family of one-way (MAC) functions that is parameterized by a symmetric key. The input to a MAC function includes a symmetric key, called *MacKey*, and a binary data string, called *MacData*. A MAC function is represented as MAC(*MacKey*, *MacData* {, ...})[12]. In this Recommendation, a MAC function is used in key confirmation (see Section 5.6) and may be used for key derivation (see Section 5.5 and SP 800-56C).

It must be computationally infeasible to determine the MAC of a (newly formed) *MacData* value without knowledge of the *MacKey* value (even if one has seen the MACs corresponding to other *MacData* values that were computed using that same *MacKey* value).

Key confirmation requires the use of one of the following **approved** MAC algorithms: HMAC, AES-CMAC or KMAC. HMAC is specified in FIPS 198 and requires the use of an **approved** hash function. AES-CMAC is specified in SP 800-38B[13] for the AES block cipher algorithm specified in FIPS 197. KMAC is specified in SP 800-185.[14]

When used for key confirmation, the key-confirmation provider is required to compute a "MAC tag" on received or derived data using the agreed-upon MAC function. A symmetric key derived from a shared secret (during a key-agreement transaction) or extracted from transported keying material (during a key-transport transaction) is used as *MacKey*. The resulting MAC tag is sent to the key-confirmation recipient, who can obtain assurance (via MAC-tag verification) that the shared secret and derived keying material were correctly computed (in the case of key agreement) or that the transported keying material was successfully received (in the case of key transport). MAC-tag computation and verification are defined in Sections 5.2.1 and 5.2.2.

---

[10] FIPS 180, *Secure Hash Standard (SHS)*.

[11] FIPS 202, *Permutation-Based Hash and Extendable-Output Functions*.

[12] Some MAC algorithms (e.g., KMAC) have additional parameters other than *MacKey* and *MacData*.

[13] SP 800-38B, *Recommendation for Block Cipher Modes of Operation: the CMAC Mode for Authentication*.

[14] SP 800-185, *SHA-3 Derived Funcions: cSHAKE, KMAC, TupleHash and ParallelHash*.

5.2.1 *MacTag* Computation for Key Confirmation

The computation of a MAC tag is represented as follows:

$$MacTag = T_{MacTagBits}[\text{MAC}(MacKey, MacData)].$$

To compute a MAC tag:

1. An **approved**, agreed-upon MAC algorithm (see FIPS 198, SP 800-38B or SP 800-185) is used with *MacKey* to compute a MAC on the *MacData*, where *MacKey* is a symmetric key, and *MacData* represents the data on which the MAC tag is computed. The minimum length of *MacKey* is specified in Section 5.6.3.

    MacKey is obtained from the *DerivedKeyingMaterial* (when a key-agreement scheme employs key confirmation) or obtained from the *TransportedKeyingMaterial* (when a key-transport scheme employs key confirmation), as specified in Section 5.6.1.1.

    The resulting MAC consists of *MacOutputBits* bits, which is the full output length of the selected MAC algorithm.

2. The output of the MAC algorithm is input to a truncation function $T_{MacTagBits}$ to obtain the most significant (i.e., leftmost) *MacTagBits* bits, where *MacTagBits* represents the intended length of *MacTag*, which is required to be less than or equal to *MacOutputBits*. (When *MacTagBits* equals *MacOutputBits*, $T_{MacTagBits}$ acts as the identity function.) The minimum value for *MacTagBits* is specified in Section 5.6.3.

Note: A routine implementing a Mac-tag computation for key confirmation **shall** destroy any local copies of *MacKey* and *MacData*, any locally stored portions of *MacTag*, and any other locally stored values used or produced during the execution of the routine; their destruction **shall** occur prior to or during any exit from the routine – whether exiting early because of an error or exiting normally with *MacTag* as the output.

5.2.2 *MacTag* Verification for Key Confirmation

To verify the MAC tag received during key confirmation, a new MAC tag, *MacTag'*, is computed as specified in Section 5.2.1 using the values of *MacKey*, *MacTagBits*, and *MacData* possessed by the key-confirmation recipient. *MacTag'* is compared with the received MAC tag (i.e., *MacTag*). If their values are equal, then it may be inferred that the same *MacKey*, *MacTagBits*, and *MacData* values were used in the computation of *MacTag* and *MacTag'*. That is, successful verification provides evidence that the key-confirmation provider has obtained the same MAC key as the key-confirmation recipient.

5.3   Random Bit Generators

Whenever this Recommendation requires the use of a randomly generated value (for example, for obtaining keys or nonces), the values **shall** be generated using an **approved** random bit generator (RBG), as specified in SP 800-90,[15] that supports an appropriate security strength.

---

[15] SP 800-90, *Recommendation for Random Number Generation.*

When an **approved** RBG is used to generate a secret value as part of a key-establishment scheme specified in this Recommendation (e.g., Z in a scheme from the KAS1 family), that RBG **shall** be instantiated to support a security strength that is equal to or greater than the security strength associated with the RSA modulus length as specified in SP 800-57, Part 1.

5.4 Nonces

A nonce is a time-varying value that has a negligible chance of repeating (where the meaning of "negligible" may be application specific). This Recommendation requires party V to supply a nonce, N_V, during the execution of key-agreement schemes in the KAS1 family (see Section 8.2). This nonce is included in the input to the key-derivation process, and (when key confirmation is employed) is also used in the computation of the MAC tag sent from party V to party U.

A nonce may be composed of one (or more) of the following components (other components may also be appropriate):

1. A random bit string that is generated anew for each nonce, using an **approved** random bit generator. A nonce containing a component of this type is called a *random nonce*.

2. A timestamp of sufficient resolution (detail) so that it is different each time that it is used.

3. A monotonically increasing sequence number, or

4. A combination of a timestamp and a monotonically increasing sequence number such that the sequence number is reset when and only when the timestamp changes. (For example, a timestamp may show the date but not the time of day, so a sequence number is appended that will not repeat during a particular day.)

For the KAS1 schemes, the required nonce N_V **should** be a random nonce containing a random bit string output from an **approved** random bit generator (RBG), where both the security strength supported by the instantiation of the random bit generator and the bit length of the random bit string are greater than or equal to the targeted security strength of the key-agreement scheme in which the nonce is used; when feasible, the bit length of the random bit string **should** be (at least) twice the targeted security strength. For details concerning the security strength supported by an instantiation of a random bit generator, see SP 800-90.

As part of the proper implementation of this Recommendation, system users and/or agents trusted to act on their behalf **should** determine that the components selected for inclusion in required nonces meet the security requirements of those users or agents. The application tasked with performing key establishment on behalf of a party **should** determine whether or not to proceed with a key-establishment transaction, based upon the perceived adequacy of the method(s) used to form the required nonces. Such knowledge may be explicitly provided to the application in some manner, or may be implicitly provided by the operation of the application itself.

5.5 Key-Derivation Methods for Key-Establishment Schemes

An **approved** key-derivation method **shall** be used to derive keying material from the shared secret Z during the execution of a key-establishment scheme from the KAS1 or KAS2 family of schemes. The shared secret **shall** be used only by an **approved** key-derivation method and **shall not** be used for any other purpose.

When employed during the execution of a key-establishment scheme as specified in this Recommendation, the agreed-upon key-derivation method uses input that includes a freshly created shared secret Z along with other information. The derived keying material **shall** be computed in its entirety before outputting any portion of it, and (all copies of) Z **shall** be treated as a critical security parameter (in a cryptographic module that is compliant with FIPS 140) and destroyed immediately following its use.

The output produced by a key-derivation method using input that includes the shared secret created during the execution of any key-establishment scheme specified in this Recommendation **shall** only be used as secret keying material – such as a symmetric key used for data encryption or message integrity, a secret initialization vector, or, perhaps, a key-derivation key that will be used to generate additional keying material (possibly using a different process – see SP 800-108[16]). The derived keying material **shall not** be used as a key stream for a stream cipher. Non-secret keying material (such as a non-secret initialization vector) **shall not** be generated using a key-derivation method that includes the shared secret, Z, as input (this restriction applies to all one-step and two-step key-derivation methods in SP 800-56C).

5.5.1 Performing the Key Derivation

Approved methods for key derivation from a shared secret are specified in SP 800-56C. These methods can be accessed using the following call:

$$\mathrm{KDM}(Z, \textit{OtherInput}),$$

where

1. Z is a byte string that represents the shared secret,

2. *OtherInput* consists of additional input information that may be required by a given key-derivation method, for example:

   - L – an integer that indicates the bit length of the secret keying material to be derived,

   - *salt* – a byte string,

   - IV – a bit string used as an initialization value, and

   - *FixedInfo* – a bit sting of context-specific data (see Section 5.5.2).

See SP 800-56C for details concerning the appropriate form of *OtherInput*.

5.5.2 FixedInfo

The bit string *FixedInfo* **should** be used to ensure that the derived keying material is adequately "bound" to the context of the key-establishment transaction. Although other methods may be used to bind keying material to the transaction context, this Recommendation makes no statement as to the adequacy of these other methods. Failure to adequately bind the derived keying material to the transaction context could adversely affect the types of assurance that can be provided by certain key-establishment schemes.

---

[16] SP 800-108, *Recommendation for Key Derivation Using Pseudorandom Functions*.

Context-specific information that may be appropriate for inclusion in *FixedInfo* includes the following:

- Public information about parties U and V, such as names, e-mail addresses, and/or other identifiers.

- The public keys contributed by each party to the key-establishment transaction. (For example, a certificate that contains the public key could be included.)

- An identifier and/or other information associated with the RSA public key employed in the key-establishment transaction. For example, the hash of a certificate that contains that RSA public key could be included.

- Other public and/or private information shared between parties U and V before or during the transaction, such as nonces, counters, or pre-shared secret data. (The inclusion of private or secret information **shall** be limited to situations in which that information is afforded adequate confidentiality protection.)

- An indication of the protocol or application employing the key-establishment scheme.

- Protocol-related information, such as a label or session identifier.

- Agreed-upon encodings (as bit strings) of the values of one or more of the other parameters used as additional input to the KDM (e.g., *L*, *salt*, and/or *IV*).

- An indication of the key-establishment scheme and/or key-derivation method used during the transaction.

- An indication of various parameter or primitive choices (e.g., hash functions, MAC algorithms, *MacTag* lengths used for key confirmation, etc.).

- An indication of how the keying material should be parsed, including an indication of which algorithm(s) will use the (parsed) keying material.

For rationale in support of including entity identifiers, scheme identifiers, and/or other information in *OtherInput*, see Appendix B of SP 800-56A.

When *FixedInfo* is used, the meaning of each information item and each item's position within the *FixedInfo* bit string **shall** be specified. In addition, each item of information included in *FixedInfo* **shall** be unambiguously represented. For example, each item of information could take the form of a fixed-length bit string, or, if greater flexibility is needed, an item of information could be represented in a *Datalen* ‖ *Data* format, where *Data* is a variable-length string of zero or more (eight-bit) bytes, and *Datalen* is a fixed-length, big-endian counter that indicates the byte length of *Data*. These requirements can be satisfied, for example, by using ASN.1 DER encoding as specified in Section 5.5.2.1.2.

5.5.2.1 One-step Key Derivation

Recommended formats for *FixedInfo* when used by a one-step key-derivation method are specified in Sections 5.5.2.1.1 and 5.5.2.1.2. One of those two formats **should** be used by a one-step key-derivation method specified in SP 800-56C when the auxiliary function employed is H = *hash*.

When *FixedInfo* is included during the key-derivation process, and the recommended formats are used, the included items of information **shall** be divided into (three, four, or five) subfields as defined below.

AlgorithmID: A required non-null subfield that indicates how the derived keying material will be parsed and for which algorithm(s) the derived secret keying material will be used. For example, *AlgorithmID* might indicate that bits 1 to 112 are to be used as a 112-bit HMAC key and that bits 113 to 240 are to be used as a 128-bit AES key.

PartyUInfo: A required non-null subfield containing public information about party U. At a minimum, *PartyUInfo* **shall** include ID_U, an identifier for party U, as a distinct item of information. This subfield could also include information about the public key (if any) contributed to the key-establishment transaction by party U. Although the schemes specified in the Recommendation do not require the contribution of a nonce by party U, any nonce provided by party U **should** be included in this subfield.

PartyVInfo: A required non-null subfield containing public information about party V. At a minimum, *PartyVInfo* **shall** include ID_V, an identifier for party V, as a distinct item of information. This subfield could also include information about the public key contributed to the key-establishment transaction by party V. When the key-derivation method is used in a KAS1 scheme (see Section 8.2), the nonce, N_V, supplied by party V **shall** be included in this field.

SuppPubInfo: An optional subfield that contains additional, mutually known public information (e.g., *L*, an identifier for the particular key-establishment scheme that was used to determine *Z*, an indication of the protocol or application employing that scheme, a session identifier, etc.; this is particularly useful if these aspects of the key-establishment transaction can vary). While an implementation may be capable of including this subfield, the subfield may be *Null* for a given transaction.

SuppPrivInfo: An optional subfield that contains additional, mutually known private information (e.g., a secret symmetric key that has been communicated through a separate channel). While an implementation may be capable of including this subfield, the subfield may be *Null* for a given transaction.

5.5.2.1.1 The Concatenation Format for *FixedInfo*

This section specifies the concatenation format for *FixedInfo*. This format has been designed to provide a simple means of binding the derived keying material to the context of the key-establishment transaction, independent of other actions taken by the relying application. Note: When the one-step key-derivation method specified in SP 800-56C is used with H = *hash* as the auxiliary function and this concatenation format for *FixedInfo*, the resulting key-derivation method is the Concatenation Key-Derivation Function specified in the original version of SP 800-56A.

For this format, *FixedInfo* is a bit string equal to the following concatenation:

> *AlgorithmID* || *PartyUInfo* || *PartyVInfo* {|| *SuppPubInfo* } {|| *SuppPrivInfo* },

where the five subfields are bit strings comprised of items of information as described in Section 5.5.2.1.

Each of the three required subfields *AlgorithmID*, *PartyUInfo*, and *PartyVInfo* **shall** be the concatenation of a pre-determined sequence of substrings in which each substring represents a distinct item of information. Each such substring **shall** have one of these two formats: either it is a fixed-length bit string, or it has the form *Datalen* || *Data* – where *Data* is a variable-length string of zero or more (eight-bit) bytes, and *Datalen* is a fixed-length, big-endian counter that indicates the byte length of *Data*. (In this variable-length format, a null string of data **shall** be represented by a zero value for *Datalen*, indicating the absence of following data.) A protocol using this format for *FixedInfo* **shall** specify the number, ordering and meaning of the information-bearing substrings that are included in each of the subfields (i.e., *AlgorithmID*, *PartyUInfo*, and *PartyVInfo*), and **shall** also specify which of the two formats (fixed-length or variable-length) is used by each such substring to represent its distinct item of information. The protocol **shall** specify the lengths for all fixed-length quantities, including the *Datalen* counters.

Each of the optional *SuppPrivInfo* and *SuppPubInfo* subfields (when allowed by the protocol employing the one-step key-derivation method) **shall** be the concatenation of a pre-determined sequence of substrings representing additional items of information that may be used during key derivation upon mutual agreement of parties U and V. Each substring representing an item of information **shall** be of the form *Datalen* || *Data*, where *Data* is a variable-length string of zero or more (eight-bit) bytes, and *Datalen* is a fixed-length, big-endian counter that indicates the byte length of *Data*; the use of this form for the information allows U and V to omit a particular information item without confusion about the meaning of the other information that is provided in the *SuppPrivInfo* or *SuppPubInfo* subfield. The substrings representing items of information that parties U and V choose not to contribute are set equal to *Null*, and are represented in this variable-length format by setting *Datalen* equal to zero. If a protocol allows the use of the *FixedInfo* subfield *SuppPrivInfo* and/or the subfield *SuppPubInfo*, then the protocol **shall** specify the number, ordering and meaning of additional items of information that may be used in the allowed subfield(s) and **shall** specify the fixed-length of the *Datalen* counters.

5.5.2.1.2   The ASN.1 Format for *FixedInfo*

The ASN.1 format for *FixedInfo* provides an alternative means of binding the derived keying material to the context of the key-establishment transaction, independent of other actions taken by the relying application. Note: When the one-step key-derivation method specified in SP 800-56C is used with H = *hash* as the auxiliary function and with this ASN.1 format for *FixedInfo*, the resulting key-derivation method is the ASN.1 Key-Derivation Function specified in the original version of SP 800-56B.

For the ASN.1 format, *FixedInfo* is a bit string resulting from the ASN.1 Distinguished Encoding Rules (DER) encoding (see ISO/IEC 8825-1) of a data structure comprised of a sequence of three required subfields *AlgorithmID*, *PartyUInfo*, and *PartyVInfo*, and, optionally, a subfield *SuppPubInfo* and/or a subfield *SuppPrivInfo* – as described in Section 5.5.2.1. A protocol using this format for *FixedInfo* **shall** specify the type, ordering and number of distinct items of information included in each of the (three, four, or five) subfields employed.

5.5.2.2   Two-step Key-Derivation (Extraction-then-Expansion)

For the two-step key-derivation method specified in SP 800-56C, *FixedInfo* is a bit string that contains component data fields such as a *Label*, *Context* information, and $[L]_2$, where:

- *Label* is a binary string that identifies the purpose of the derived keying material. The encoding method for the label is defined in a larger context, for example, in a protocol using the derivation method.

- *Context* is a binary string containing information relating to the derived keying material. Section 5.5.2 provides a list of context-specific information that may be appropriate for the inclusion in this string.

- $[L]_2$ is a binary string that specifies the length (in bits) of the keying material to be derived.

Different orderings of the component data fields of *FixedInfo* may be used, and one or more of the data fields may be combined (or omitted under certain circumstances). See SP 800-108 and Section 5 in SP 800-56C for details.

5.5.2.3 Other Formats for *FixedInfo*

Formats other than those provided in Sections 5.5.2.1 and 5.5.2.2 (e.g., those providing the items of information in a different arrangement) may be used for *FixedInfo*, but the context-specific information described in the preceding sections **should** be included (see the discussion in Section 5.5.2). This Recommendation makes no statement as to the adequacy of other formats.

5.6   Key Confirmation

The term key confirmation (KC) refers to actions taken to provide assurance to one party (the key-confirmation recipient) that another party (the key-confirmation provider) is in possession of a (supposedly) shared secret and/or to confirm that the other party has the correct version of keying material that was derived or transported during a key-establishment transaction (correct, that is, from the perspective of the key-confirmation recipient.) Such actions are said to provide unilateral key confirmation when they provide this assurance to only one of the participants in the key-establishment transaction; the actions are said to provide bilateral key confirmation when this assurance is provided to both participants (i.e., when unilateral key confirmation is provided in both directions).

Oftentimes, key confirmation is obtained (at least implicitly) by some means that are external to the key-establishment scheme employed during a transaction (e.g., by using a symmetric key that was established during the transaction to decrypt an encrypted message sent later by the key-confirmation provider), but this is not always the case. In some circumstances, it may be appropriate to incorporate the exchange of explicit key-confirmation information as an integral part of the key-establishment scheme itself. The inclusion of key confirmation may enhance the security services that can be offered by a key-establishment scheme. For example, the key-establishment schemes incorporating key confirmation that are specified in this Recommendation could be used to provide the KC recipient with assurance that the KC provider is in possession of the private key corresponding to the provider's public key-establishment key, from which the recipient may infer that the provider is the owner of that key pair.

For key confirmation to comply with this Recommendation, key confirmation **shall** be incorporated into an **approved** key-establishment scheme as specified in Sections 5.6.1, 5.6.2, 8 and 9. If any other methods are used to provide key confirmation, this Recommendation makes no statement as to their adequacy.

5.6.1 Unilateral Key Confirmation for Key-Establishment Schemes

As specified in this Recommendation, unilateral key confirmation occurs when one participant in the execution of a key-establishment scheme (the key-confirmation "provider") demonstrates to the satisfaction of the other participant (the key-confirmation "recipient") that both the KC provider and the KC recipient have possession of the same secret *MacKey*.

MacKey **shall** be a symmetric key that is unique to a specific execution of a key-establishment scheme and (from the perspective of the KC provider) **shall** be unpredictable prior to that key-establishment transaction. In the case of a key-agreement scheme, *MacKey* is derived using the shared secret *Z* created during the execution of that scheme (see Section 5.5 for the details of key derivation). In the case of a key-transport scheme, *MacKey* is included as part of the transported keying material. Step 2 below specifies how *MacKey* is to be extracted from the derived or transported keying material.

MacKey and certain context-specific *MacData* (as specified below) are used by the KC provider as input to an **approved** MAC algorithm to obtain a MAC tag that is sent to the KC recipient. The recipient performs an independent computation of the MAC tag. If the MAC tag value computed by the KC recipient matches the MAC tag value received from the KC provider, then key confirmation is successful. (See Section 5.2 for MAC-tag generation and verification, and Section 5.6.3 for a discussion of MAC-tag security.)

In the case of a scheme providing key-agreement, successful key confirmation following key agreement provides assurance to the KC recipient that the same *Z* value has been used by both parties to correctly derive the keying material (which includes *MacKey*). In the case of a key-transport scheme (see Section 9.2.4), successful key confirmation provides assurance to the KC recipient (who sent the keying material) that the transported keying material (which includes *MacKey*) has been correctly decrypted by the party to whom it was sent.

A close examination of the KC process shows that each of the pair-wise key-establishment schemes specified in this Recommendation that incorporate key confirmation can be used to provide the KC recipient with assurance that the KC provider is currently in possession of the (correct) private key – the one corresponding to the KC provider's public key-establishment key. The use of transaction-specific values for both *MacKey* and *MacData* prevents (for all practical purposes) the replay of any previously computed value of *MacTag*. The receipt of a correctly computed MAC tag provides assurance to the KC recipient that the KC provider has used the correct private key during the current transaction – to successfully recover the secret data that is a prerequisite to learning the value of *MacKey*.

To include unilateral key confirmation, the following steps **shall** be incorporated into the scheme. (Additional details will be provided for each scheme in the appropriate subsections of Sections 8 and 9.) In the discussion that follows, the key-confirmation provider, P, may be either party U or party V, as long as the KC provider, P, contributes a key pair to the key-establishment transaction. The key-confirmation recipient, R, is the other party.

1. The provider, P, computes

    $$MacData_P = message\_string_P \parallel ID_P \parallel ID_R \parallel EphemData_P \parallel EphemData_R \{\parallel Text_P\}$$

    where

- *message_string$_P$* is a six-byte character string, with a value of "KC_1_U" when party U is providing the MAC tag, or "KC_1_V" when party V is providing the MAC tag. (Note that these values will be changed for bilateral key confirmation, as specified in Section 5.6.2).

- *ID$_P$* is the identifier used to label the key-confirmation provider.

- *ID$_R$* is the identifier used to label the key-confirmation recipient.

- *EphemData$_P$* and *EphemData$_R$* are (ephemeral) values contributed by the KC provider and recipient, respectively. These values are specified in the sections describing the schemes that include key confirmation.

- *Text$_P$* is an optional bit string that may be used during key confirmation and that is known by both parties.

The content of each of the components that are concatenated to form *MacData$_P$* **shall** be precisely defined and unambiguously represented. A particular component's content may be represented, for example, as a fixed-length bit string or in the form *Datalen* ‖ *Data*, where *Data* is a variable-length string of zero or more (eight-bit) bytes, and *Datalen* is a fixed-length, big-endian counter that indicates the length (in bytes) of *Data*. These requirements could also be satisfied by using a specific ASN.1 DER encoding of each component. It is imperative that the provider and recipient have agreed upon the content and format that will be used for each component of *MacData$_P$*.

MacData **shall** include a non-null identifier, *ID$_P$*, for the key-confirmation provider.

Depending upon the circumstances, the key-confirmation recipient's identifier, *ID$_R$*, may be replaced by a null string. The rules for selecting *ID$_P$* and *ID$_R$* are as follows:

As specified in this Recommendation, the key-confirmation provider must own a key pair that is employed by the basic key-establishment scheme (**KAS1-basic, KAS2-basic** or **KTS-OAEP-basic)** that determines the *MacKey* value used in the key-confirmation computations performed during the transaction. The identifier, *ID$_p$*, included in *MacData$_P$* **shall** be one that has a trusted association with the public key of that key pair.

For the KAS2 family of schemes, the identifier of the key-confirmation recipient included in *MacData$_P$* (i.e., *ID$_R$*) **shall** be one that has a trusted association with the public key of the key pair used by the key-confirmation recipient during the transaction.

If the key-confirmation recipient does not own a key pair employed for key-establishment purposes, and no identifier has been used to label that party during the execution of the basic key-establishment scheme employed by the transaction, then *ID$_R$* may be replaced by a null string. However, if an identifier is desired/required for that party for key confirmation purposes, then a non-null value for *ID$_R$*, **shall** be selected/assigned in accordance with the requirements of the protocol relying upon the transaction.

Whenever a particular identifier has been used to label the key-confirmation recipient or key-confirmation provider in the execution of the basic key-establishment scheme used during the transaction, that same identifier **shall** be used as ID_P or ID_R, respectively, in the *MacData$_P$* used during key confirmation. For example, if party U is the key-confirmation recipient, and ID_U has been used to label party U in the *FixedInfo* employed by the key-derivation method of a key-agreement scheme used during the transaction, then the *MacData$_P$* used during key confirmation **shall** have $ID_R = ID_U$.

2. When a **KAS1** or **KAS2** key-agreement scheme is used: After computing the shared secret Z and applying the key-derivation function to obtain the derived keying material, *DerivedKeyingMaterial* (see Section 5.5), the KC provider uses agreed-upon bit lengths to parse *DerivedKeyingMaterial* into two parts, *MacKey* and *KeyData*:

$$DerivedKeyingMaterial = MacKey \parallel KeyData.$$

When the **KTS-OAEP** key-transport scheme is used: The KC provider parses the *TransportedKeyingMaterial* into *MacKey* and *KeyData*:

$$TransportedKeyingMaterial = MacKey \parallel KeyData.$$

3. Using an agreed-upon bit length *MacTagBits,* the KC provider computes *MacTag$_P$* (see Sections 5.2.1 and 5.6.3):

$$MacTag_P = T_{MacTagBits}[\text{MAC } (MacKey, MacData_P)],$$

and sends it to the KC recipient.

4. The KC recipient forms *MacData$_P$,* determines *MacKey*, computes *MacTag$_P$* in the same manner as the KC provider, and then compares its computed *MacTag$_P$* to the value received from the provider. If the received value is equal to the computed value, then the recipient is assured that the provider has used the same value for *MacKey* and that the provider shares the recipient's value of *MacTag$_P$*.

Each participant **shall** destroy all copies of the *MacKey* that was employed for key-confirmation purposes during a particular pair-wise key-establishment transaction when *MacKey* is no longer needed to provide or obtain key confirmation as part of that transaction.

If *MacTag$_P$* cannot be verified by the KC recipient during a particular key-establishment transaction, then key confirmation has failed, and both participants **shall** destroy all of their copies of *MacKey* and *KeyData*. In particular, *MacKey* and *KeyData* **shall not** be revealed by either participant to any other party (not even to the other participant), and the keying material **shall not** be used for any further purpose. In the case of a key-confirmation failure, the key-establishment transaction **shall** be terminated.

Note: The key-confirmation routines employed by the KC provider and KC recipient **shall** destroy all local copies of *MacKey, MacData*, destroyable copies of *KeyData* and any other locally stored values used or produced during the execution of those routines. The destruction of those locally stored values **shall** occur prior to or during any exit from those routines – whether exiting normally or exiting early, because of an error.

Unilateral key confirmation, as specified in this Recommendation, can be incorporated into any key-establishment scheme in which the key-confirmation provider is required to own a key-establishment key pair that is used in the key-establishment process. Unilateral key confirmation may be added in either direction to a **KAS2** scheme (see Sections 8.3.3.2 and 8.3.3.3); it may also be added to a **KAS1** or **KTS-OAEP** scheme, but only with party V (the party contributing the key pair) acting as the key-confirmation provider, and party U acting as the key-confirmation recipient (see Sections 8.2.3.1 and 9.2.4.2).

5.6.2 Bilateral Key Confirmation for KAS2 Schemes

Bilateral key confirmation, as specified in this Recommendation, can be incorporated into a **KAS2** key-agreement scheme since each party is required to own a key-establishment key pair that is used in the key-agreement process. Bilateral key confirmation is accomplished by performing unilateral key confirmation in both directions (with party U providing $MacTag_U$ to KC recipient V, and party V providing $MacTag_V$ to KC recipient U) during the same scheme.

To include bilateral key confirmation, two instances of unilateral key confirmation (as specified in Section 5.6.1, subject to the modifications listed below) **shall** be incorporated into the **KAS2** scheme, once with party U as the key-confirmation provider (i.e., P = U and R = V) and once with party V as the key-confirmation provider (i.e., P = V and R = U). Additional details will be provided in Section 8.3.3.4.

In addition to setting P = U and R = V in one instance of the unilateral key-confirmation procedure described in Section 5.6.1 and setting P = V and R = U in a second instance, the following changes/clarifications apply when using the procedure for bilateral key confirmation:

1. When computing $MacTag_U$, the value of $message\_string_U$ that forms the initial segment of $MacData_U$ is the six-byte character string "KC_2_U".

2. When computing $MacTag_V$, the value of $message\_string_V$ that forms the initial segment of $MacData_V$ is the six-byte character string "KC_2_V".

3. If used at all, the value of the (optional) byte string $Text_U$ used to form the final segment of $MacData_U$ can be different than the value of the (optional) byte string $Text_V$ used to form the final segment of $MacData_V$, provided that both parties are aware of the value(s) used.

4. The identifiers used to label the parties U and V when forming $MacData_U$ **shall** be the same as the identifiers used to label the parties U and V when forming $MacData_V$, although ID_U and ID_V will play different roles in the two strings. If $ID_P = ID_U$ and $ID_R = ID_V$ are used in $MacData_U$, then $ID_P = ID_V$ and $ID_R = ID_U$ are used in $MacData_V$.

5.6.3 Selecting the MAC and Other Key-Confirmation Parameters

Key confirmation as specified in this Recommendation requires that a $MacKey$ of an appropriate length be generated or obtained as part of the derived keying material (see Section 5.6.1). The $MacKey$ is then used with a MAC algorithm to generate a MAC; the length of the MAC output by the MAC algorithm is $MacOutputBits$ bits. The MAC is subsequently used to form a MAC tag (see Section 5.6.1 for the generation of the MAC and Section 5.2.1 for the formation of the MAC tag from the MAC).

Table 1 provides a list of **approved** MAC algorithms for key confirmation and the security strengths that each can support, along with the corresponding value of $MacOutputBits$ and permissible $MacKey$ lengths for each MAC algorithm.

Table 1: Approved MAC Algorithms for Key Confirmation

MAC Algorithm	*MacOutputBits*	Permissable *MacKey* Lengths (μ bits)	Supported Security Strengths for Key Confirmation (*s* bits)
HMAC-SHA-1	160		
HMAC-SHA-224	224		
HMAC-SHA-256	256		
HMAC-SHA-512/224	224		
HMAC-SHA-512/256	256		
HMAC-SHA-384	384	$s \leq \mu \leq 512$	$112 \leq s \leq 256$
HMAC-SHA-512	512		
HMAC-SHA3-224	224		
HMAC-SHA3-256	256		
HMAC-SHA3-384	384		
HMAC-SHA3-512	512		
KMAC128	$\leq 2^{2040} - 1$ (see * below)		$112 \leq s \leq 128$
KMAC256			$112 \leq s \leq 256$
AES-128-CMAC	128	$\mu = 128$	$112 \leq s \leq 128$
AES-192-CMAC	128	$\mu = 192$	$112 \leq s \leq 192$
AES-256-CMAC	128	$\mu = 256$	$112 \leq s \leq 256$

*   Although KMAC128 and KMAC256 can accommodate *MacOutputBits* values as large as $2^{2040} - 1$, practical considerations dictate that the lengths of transmitted MAC tags be limited to sizes that are more realistic and commensurate with the actual performance/security requirements of the relying applications.

The MAC algorithm used to compute a key-confirmation MAC tag in compliance with this Recommendation **shall** be selected from among the **approved** MAC algorithms capable of supporting a security strength s that is at least as large as the targeted security strength of the key-establishment scheme (as indicated in Table 1 above).

Note that when the HMAC or KMAC algorithm is used for key confirmation as specified in this Recommendation, *MacKey* lengths can be no greater than 512 bits (an upper bound that is at least twice the maximum supported security strength). Although the HMAC and KMAC specifications permit the use of longer keys, the 512-bit maximum is sufficient for this key-confirmation application. In the case of HMAC, the 512-bit upper bound has the advantage of being less than or equal to the input block length of whatever hash function is used in the algorithm's implementation. If *MacKey* were allowed to be longer than the input block length, it would be hashed down to a string of length *MacOutputBits* during the HMAC computation (see step 2 in Table 1 of FIPS 198); allowing *MacKey* to be longer than the input block length would not be an efficient use of keying material.

The length of the MAC tag for key confirmation also needs to be selected. Note that in many cases, the length of the MAC tag (*MacTagBits*) has been selected by the protocol in which the key-establishment is conducted. *MacTagBits* **shall** be at least 64 bits, and its maximum length **shall** be no more than *MacOutputBits* for the MAC algorithm selected for key confirmation. The 64-bit minimum for the MAC tag length assumes that the protocol imposes a limit on the number of retries for key confirmation.

6   RSA Key Pairs

6.1   General Requirements

The following are requirements on RSA key pairs (see SP 800-57):

1. Each key pair **shall** be created using an **approved** key-generation method as specified in Section 6.3.

2. The private keys and prime factors of the modulus **shall** be protected from unauthorized access, disclosure, and modification.

3. Public keys **shall** be protected from unauthorized modification. This is often accomplished by using public-key certificates that have been signed by a trusted Certification Authority (CA).

4. A recipient of a public key **shall** be assured of the integrity and correct association of (a) the public key and (b) an identifier of the entity that owns the key pair (that is, the party with whom the recipient intends to establish secret keying material). This assurance is often provided by verifying a public-key certificate that was signed by a trusted third party (for example, a CA), but may be provided by direct distribution of the public key and identifier from the owner, provided that the recipient trusts the owner and distribution process to do this.

5. One key pair **shall not** be used for different cryptographic purposes (for example, a digital-signature key pair **shall not** be used for key establishment or vice versa), with the following possible exception: when requesting the certificate for a public key-establishment key, the private key-establishment key associated with the public key may be used to sign the certificate request (see SP 800-57, Part 1 on Key Usage for further information). A key pair may be used in more than one key-establishment scheme. However, a key pair used for schemes specified in this Recommendation **should not** be used for any schemes not specified herein.

6. The owner of a key pair **shall** have assurance of the key pair's validity (see Section 6.4.1.1); that is, the owner **shall** have assurance of the correct generation of the key pair (see Section 6.3), consistent with the criteria of Section 6.2; assurance of private and public-key validity; and assurance of pair-wise consistency.

7. A recipient of a public key **shall** have assurance of the validity of the public key (see Section 6.4.2.1). This assurance may be provided, for example, through the use of a public-key certificate if the CA obtains sufficient assurance of public-key validity as part of its certification process.

8. A recipient of a public key **shall** have assurance of the owner's possession of the associated private key (see Section 6.4.2.3). This assurance may be provided, for example, through the use of a public key certificate if the CA obtains sufficient assurance of possession as part of its certification process.

6.2 Criteria for RSA Key Pairs for Key Establishment

6.2.1 Definition of a Key Pair

A valid RSA key pair, in its basic form, **shall** consist of an RSA public key (n, e) and an RSA private key (n, d), where:

1. n, the public modulus, **shall** be the product of exactly two distinct, odd positive prime factors, p and q, that are kept secret. Let $\mathrm{len}(n) = nBits$, the bit length of n; $\mathrm{len}(n)$ is required to be even.

2. The public exponent e **shall** be an odd integer that is selected prior to the generation of p and q such that:

$$65,537 \le e < 2^{256}$$

3. The prime factors p and q **shall** be generated using one of the methods specified in Appendix B.3 of FIPS 186 such that:

    a. $2^{(nBits - 1)/2} < p < 2^{nBits/2}$.

    b. $2^{(nBits - 1)/2} < q < 2^{nBits/2}$.

    c. $|p - q| > 2^{nBits/2 - 100}$.

    d. The exponent e must be mutually prime with both $p - 1$ and $q - 1$:

$$GCD(e, LCM(p - 1, q - 1)) = 1.$$

4. The primes p and q, and the private exponent d **shall** be selected such that:

    a. $2^{nBits/2} < d < LCM(p-1, q-1)$, and

    b. $d = e^{-1} \bmod (LCM(p-1, q-1))$.

    Regarding step 4a: One can be certain that the inequality $2^{nBits/2} < d$ will be satisfied even before d is computed by verifying that $LCM(p-1, q-1) \ge (e)(2^{nBits/2})$. The second inequality, $d < LCM(p-1, q-1)$, will be satisfied if d is computed as specified in step b).

Note that these criteria are also specified in FIPS 186.

6.2.2 Formats

The RSA private key may be expressed in several formats. The basic format of the RSA private key consists of the modulus n and a private-key exponent d that depends on n and the public-key exponent e; this format is used to specify the RSA primitives and operations in Section 7. The other two formats may be used in implementations, but may require appropriate modifications for correct implementation. To facilitate implementation testing, the format for the private key **shall** be one of the following:

1. The basic format: (n, d).

2. The prime-factor format: (p, q, d).

3. The Chinese Remainder Theorem (CRT) format: $(n, e, d, p, q, dP, dQ, qInv)$, where $dP = d \bmod (p - 1)$, $dQ = d \bmod (q - 1)$, and $qInv = q^{-1} \bmod p$. Note that Section 7.1.2 discusses the use of the private key expressed using the CRT format during the execution of the RSA decryption primitive.

Key-pair generators and key-pair validation methods are given for each of these formats in Sections 6.3 and 6.4, respectively.

6.3   RSA Key-Pair Generators

The key pairs employed by the key-establishment schemes specified in this Recommendation **shall** be generated using the techniques specified in Appendix B.3 of FIPS 186, employing the requisite methods for prime-number generation, primality testing, etc., that are specified in Appendix C of that document. Note that these generation methods ensure that the prime factors p and q have the same bit length and that their product, n (the RSA modulus), has a bit length that is exactly twice the length of its factors.

An **approved** RSA key-pair generator and **approved** random bit generator (RBG) **shall** be used to produce an RSA key pair. Any modulus with an even bit length that provides at least 112 bits of security strength may be used. Commonly used modulus lengths and their associated security strengths are given in Table 2. For other modulus lengths, Appendix D provides a method for estimating the security strength that can be supported.

Table 2: Security Strengths Supported by Commonly Used Modulus Lengths[17]

Modulus Bit length (*nBits*)	Estimated Maximum Security Strength
2048	112
3072	128
4096	152
6144	176
8192	200

Approved RBGs are discussed in Section 5.3. The **approved** RSA key-pair generators are provided in Sections 6.3.1 and 6.3.2, and are differentiated by the method for determining the public-key exponent e that is used as part of an RSA public key (i.e., (n, e)); Section 6.3.1 addresses the use of a fixed value for the exponent, whereas Section 6.3.2 uses a randomly generated value.

For the following methods in Section 6.3 and the assurances in Section 6.4, let ES(*nBits*) denote the estimated maximum security strength for a modulus of bit length *nBits* as determined by Table 2 or Appendix D.

---

[17] The 15,384-bit modulus length was not included because it is impractical to implement.

6.3.1 RSAKPG1 Family: RSA Key-Pair Generation with a Fixed Public Exponent

The RSAKPG1 family of key-pair generation methods consists of three RSA key-pair generators where the public exponent has a fixed value (see Section 6.2).

Three representations are addressed:

1. *rsakpg1-basic* generates the private key in the basic format (n, d);

2. *rsakpg1-prime-factor* generates the private key in the prime-factor format (p, q, d); and

3. *rsakpg1-crt* generates the private key in the Chinese Remainder Theorem format $(n, e, d, p, q, dP, dQ, qInv)$.

An implementation may perform a key-pair validation before the key pair is output from the generator. The key-pair validation methods for this family are specified in Section 6.4.1.2.

6.3.1.1 *rsakpg1-basic*

rsakpg1-basic is the generator in the RSAKPG1 family where the private key is in the basic format (n, d).

Function call: *rsakpg1-basic(s, nBits, e)*
Input:
1. s: the targeted security strength;

2. *nBits*: the intended bit length of the RSA modulus; and

3. e: a pre-determined public exponent – an odd integer, such that $65{,}537 \le e < 2^{256}$.

Process:
1. Check the values:

   a. If s is not in the range [112, 256], output an indication that the targeted security strength is not acceptable, and exit without further processing.

   b. If $s > \text{ES}(nBits)$, output an indication that the modulus length is not adequate for the targeted security strength, and exit without further processing.

   c. If e is not an odd integer such that $65{,}537 \le e < 2^{256}$, output an indication that the exponent is out of range, and exit without further processing.

2. Generate the prime factors p and q, as specified in FIPS 186. Note that the routines ensure that $p - 1$ and $q - 1$ are relatively prime to e.

3. Determine the private exponent d:

$$d = e^{-1} \bmod \text{LCM}(p - 1, q - 1).$$

   In the very rare event that $d \le 2^{nBits/2}$, discard the results of all computations and repeat the process, starting at step 2.

4. Determine the modulus n as $n = p \times q$, the product of p and q.

5. Perform a pair-wise consistency test[18] by verifying that m is the same as $(m^e)^d \bmod n$ for some integer m satisfying $1 < m < (n-1)$. If an inconsistency is found, output an indication of a pair-wise consistency failure, and exit without further processing.

6. Output (n, e) as the public key, and (n, d) as the private key.

Output:

1. (n, e): the RSA public key, and

2. (n, d): the RSA private key in the basic format.

Errors: Indications of the following:

1. The targeted security strength is not acceptable,

2. The intended modulus bit length is not adequate for the targeted security strength,

3. The fixed public exponent is out of range, or

4. Pair-wise consistency failure.

Note that key-pair validation, as specified in Section 6.4.1.2.1, can be performed after step 5 and before step 6 of the process above. If an error is detected during the validation process, output an indication of a key-pair validation failure, and exit without further processing.

A routine that implements this generation function **shall** destroy any local copies of p, q, and d, as well as any other locally stored values used or produced during the execution of the routine. The destruction of these locally stored values **shall** occur prior to or during any exit from the routine (whether exiting early because of an error, or exiting normally with the output of an RSA key pair). Note that the requirement for destruction includes any locally stored portions of the output key pair.

6.3.1.2 *rsakpg1-prime-factor*

rsakpg1-prime-factor is the generator in the RSAKPG1 family such that the private key is in the prime factor format (p, q, d).

Function call: *rsakpg1-prime-factor(s, nBits, e)*

The inputs, outputs and errors are the same as in *rsakpg1-basic* (see Section 6.3.1.1) except that the private key is in the prime-factor format: (p, q, d).

The steps are the same as in *rsakpg1-basic* except that processing Step 6 is replaced by the following:

6. Output (n, e) as the public key, and (p, q, d) as the private key.

---

[18] Although the previous steps should have theoretically produced a valid key pair, this step is required to ensure that implementation errors do not result in an invalid key pair.

Note that key-pair validation, as specified in Section 6.4.1.2.2, can be performed after step 5 and before step 6. If an error is detected during the validation process, output an indication of a key-pair validation failure, and exit without further processing.

A routine that implements this generation function **shall** destroy any local copies of p, q, and d, as well as any other locally stored values used or produced during the execution of the routine. The destruction of these locally stored values **shall** occur prior to or during any exit from the routine (whether exiting early, because of an error, or exiting normally, with the output of an RSA key pair). Note that the requirement for destruction includes any locally stored portions of the output key pair.

6.3.1.3 *rsakpg1-crt*

rsakpg1-crt is the generator in the RSAKPG1 family such that the private key is in the Chinese Remainder Theorem format $(n, e, d, p, q, dP, dQ, qInv)$.

Function call: *rsakpg1-crt*(s, $nBits$, e)

The inputs, outputs and errors are the same as in *rsakpg1-basic* (see Section 6.3.1.1) except that the private key is in the Chinese Remainder Theorem format: $(n, e, d, p, q, dP, dQ, qInv)$.

The steps are the same as in *rsakpg1-basic* except that processing steps 5 and 6 are replaced by the following:

5. Determine the components dP, dQ and $qInv$:

    a. $dP = d \bmod (p - 1)$.

    b. $dQ = d \bmod (q - 1)$.

    c. $qInv = q^{-1} \bmod p$.

6. Perform a pair-wise consistency test[19] by verifying that $m = (m^e)^d \bmod n$ for some integer m satisfying $1 < m < (n - 1)$. If an inconsistency is found, output an indication of a pair-wise consistency failure, and exit without further processing.

7. Output (n, e) as the public key, and $(n, e, d, p, q, dP, dQ, qInv)$ as the private key.

Note that key-pair validation, as specified in Section 6.4.1.2.3, can be performed after step 6 and before step 7. If an error is detected during the validation process, output an indication of a key-pair validation failure, and exit without further processing.

A routine that implements this generation function **shall** destroy any local copies of p, q, dP, dQ, $qInv$, and d, as well as any other locally stored values used or produced during the execution of the routine. The destruction of these locally stored values **shall** occur prior to or during any exit from the routine (whether exiting early because of an error or exiting normally with the output of an RSA key pair). Note that the requirement for destruction includes any locally stored portions of the output key pair.

---

[19] Although the previous steps should have theoretically produced a valid key pair, this step is required to ensure that implementation errors do not result in an invalid key pair.

6.3.2 RSAKPG2 Family: RSA Key-Pair Generation with a Random Public Exponent

The RSAKPG2 family of key-pair generation methods consists of three RSA key-pair generators such that the public exponent e is a random value in the range $65{,}537 \le e < 2^{256}$.

Three representations are addressed:

1. *rsakpg2-basic* generates the private key in the basic format (n, d);

2. *rsakpg2-prime-factor* generates the private key in the prime factor format (p, q, d); and

3. *rsakpg2-crt* generates the private key in the Chinese Remainder Theorem format $(n, e, d, p, q, dP, dQ, qInv)$.

An implementation may perform a key-pair validation before outputting the key pair from the generation function. The key-pair validation methods for this family are specified in Section 6.4.1.3.

6.3.2.1 *rsakpg2-basic*

rsakpg2-basic is the generator in the RSAKPG2 family such that the private key is in the basic format (n, d).

Function call: *rsakpg2-basic*(s, *nBits*, *eBits*)

Input:

1. s: the targeted security strength;

2. *nBits*: the intended bit length of the RSA modulus; and

3. *eBits*: the intended bit length of the public exponent – an integer such that $17 \le eBits \le 256$. Note that the public exponent **shall** be an odd integer such that $65{,}537 \le e < 2^{256}$.

Process:

1. Check the values:

   a. If s is not in the range [112, 256], output an indication that the targeted security strength is not acceptable, and exit without further processing.

   b. If $s > \text{ES}(nBits)$, output an indication that the modulus length is not adequate for the targeted security strength, and exit without further processing.

   c. If *eBits* is not an integer such that $17 \le eBits \le 256$, output an indication that the exponent length is out of range, and exit without further processing.

2. Generate an odd public exponent e in the range $[2^{eBits-1} + 1, 2^{eBits} - 1]$ using an **approved** RBG (see Section 5.3).

3. Generate the prime factors p and q as specified in FIPS 186. Note that the routines ensure that $p-1$ and $q-1$ are relatively prime to e.

4. Determine the private exponent d:

   $$d = e^{-1} \bmod \text{LCM}(p-1, q-1).$$

In the event that no such d exists, or in the very rare event that $d \leq 2^{nBits/2}$, discard the results of all computations and repeat the process, starting at step 2.

5. Determine the modulus n as $n = p \times q$, the product of p and q.

6. Perform a pair-wise consistency test[20] by verifying that m is the same as $(m^e)^d \bmod n$ for some integer m satisfying $1 < m < (n - 1)$. If an inconsistency is found, output an indication of a pair-wise consistency failure, and exit without further processing.

7. Output (n, e) as the public key and (n, d) as the private key.

Output:

1. (n, e): the RSA public key; and

2. (n, d): the RSA private key in the basic format.

Errors: Indications of the following:

1. The targeted security strength is not acceptable,

2. The intended modulus bit length is not adequate for the targeted security strength,

3. The intended exponent bit length is out of range, or

4. Pair-wise consistency failure.

Note that key-pair validation, as specified in Section 6.4.1.3.1, can be performed after step 6 and before step 7 of the process above. If an error is detected during the validation process, output an indication of a key-pair validation failure, and exit without further processing.

A routine that implements this generation function **shall** destroy any local copies of p, q, and d, as well as any other locally stored values used or produced during the execution of the routine. The destruction of these locally stored values **shall** occur prior to or during any exit from the routine (whether exiting early, because of an error, or exiting normally, with the output of an RSA key pair). Note that the requirement for destruction includes any locally stored portions of the output key pair.

6.3.2.2 *rsakpg2-prime-factor*

rsakpg2-prime-factor is the generator in the RSAKPG2 family such that the private key is in the prime-factor format (p, q, d).

Function call: *rsakpg2-prime-factor*(s, $nBits$, $eBits$)

The inputs, outputs and errors are the same as in *rsakpg2-basic* (see Section 6.3.2.1) except that the private key is in the prime-factor format: (p, q, d).

The steps are the same as in *rsakpg2-basic* except that processing Step 7 is replaced by the following:

7. Output (n, e) as the public key, and (p, q, d) as the private key.

---

[20] Although the previous steps should have theoretically produced a valid key pair, this step is required to ensure that implementation errors do not result in an invalid key pair.

Note that key-pair validation as specified in Section 6.4.1.3.2 can be performed after step 6 and before step 7. If an error is detected during the validation process, output an indication of a key-pair validation failure, and exit without further processing.

A routine that implements this generation function **shall** destroy any local copies of p, q, and d, as well as any other locally stored values used or produced during the execution of the routine. The destruction of these locally stored values **shall** occur prior to or during any exit from the routine (whether exiting early because of an error or exiting normally with the output of an RSA key pair). Note that the requirement for destruction includes any locally stored portions of the output key pair.

6.3.2.3 *rsakpg2-crt*

rsakpg2-crt is the generator in the RSAKPG2 family such that the private key is in the Chinese Remainder Theorem format $(n, e, d, p, q, dP, dQ, qInv)$.

Function call: *rsakpg2-crt*(*s*, *nBits*, *eBits*)

The inputs, outputs and errors are the same as in *rsakpg2-basic* (see Section 6.3.2.1) except that the private key is in the Chinese Remainder Theorem format: $(n, e, d, p, q, dP, dQ, qInv)$.

The steps are the same as in *rsakpg2-basic* except that processing Steps 6 and 7 are replaced by the following:

6. Determine the components dP, dQ and $qInv$:

    a. $dP = d \bmod (p - 1)$.

    b. $dQ = d \bmod (q - 1)$.

    c. $qInv = q^{-1} \bmod p$.

7. Perform a pair-wise consistency test[21] by verifying that m *is* the same as $(m^e)^d \bmod n$ for some integer m satisfying $1 < m < (n - 1)$. If an inconsistency is found, output an indication of a pair-wise consistency failure, and exit without further processing.

8. Output (n, e) as the public key, and $(n, e, d, p, q, dP, dQ, qInv)$ as the private key.

Note that key-pair validation as specified in Section 6.4.1.3.3 can be performed after step 7 and before step 8. If an error is detected during the validation process, output an indication of a key-pair validation failure, and exit without further processing.

A routine that implements this generation function **shall** destroy any local copies of p, q, dP, dQ, $qInv$, and d, as well as any other locally stored values used or produced during the execution of the routine. The destruction of these locally stored values **shall** occur prior to or during any exit from the routine (whether exiting early because of an error, or exiting normally with the output of an RSA key pair). Note that the requirement for destruction includes any locally stored portions of the output key pair.

---

[21] Although the previous steps should have theoretically produced a valid key pair, this step is required to ensure that implementation errors do not result in an invalid key pair.

6.4   Required Assurances

Secure key establishment depends upon the use of valid key-establishment keys. The security of key-establishment schemes also depends on limiting knowledge of the private keys to those who have been authorized to use them (i.e., their respective owners) and to the trusted third party that may have generated them.[22] In addition to preventing unauthorized entities from gaining access to private keys, it is also important that owners have possession of the correct private keys.

To explain the assurance requirements, some terminology needs to be defined. The owner of a key pair is the entity that is authorized to use the private key that corresponds to the owner's public key, whether or not the owner generated the key pair. The recipient of a public key is the entity that is participating in a key-establishment transaction with the owner and obtains the owner's public key before or during the current transaction.

Prior to or during a key-establishment transaction, the participants in the transaction (i.e., parties U and V) **shall** obtain the appropriate assurances about the key pairs used during that transaction. The types of assurance that may be sought by one or both of the parties (U and/or V) concerning the components of a key pair (i.e., the private key and public key) are discussed in Sections 6.4.1 and 6.4.2.

6.4.1 Assurances Required by the Key-Pair Owner

Prior to the use of a key pair in a key-establishment transaction, the key-pair owner **shall** have assurance of the validity of the key pair. Assurance of key-pair validity provides assurance that a key pair was generated in accordance with the requirements in Sections 6.2 and 6.3. Key-pair validity implies public-key validity and assurance of possession of the correct private key. Assurance of key-pair validity can only be provided by an entity that has the private key (e.g., the owner). Depending on an organization's requirements, a renewal of key-pair validity may be prudent. The method of obtaining initial and renewed assurance of key-pair validity is addressed in Section 6.4.1.1.

Assurance of key-pair validity can be renewed at any time (see Section 6.4.1.1). As time passes, an owner may lose possession of the correct value of the private-key component of their key pair, e.g., due to an error; for this reason, renewed (i.e., current) assurance of possession of a private key can be of value for some applications. See Section 6.4.1.5 for techniques that the owner can use to obtain renewed assurance of private-key possession separately from assurance of key-pair validity.

6.4.1.1 Obtaining Owner Assurance of Key-Pair Validity

Assurance of key-pair validity **shall** be obtained by its owner prior to the first use of the key pair in a key-establishment transaction (see Section 4.1) by successfully completing the following three-step process:

---

[22] The trusted third party is trusted not to use or reveal the distributed private keys.

1. Key-pair generation: Assurance that the key pair has been correctly formed, in a manner consistent with the criteria of Section 6.2, is obtained using one of the following two methods:

   a. Owner generation – The owner obtains the desired assurance if it generates the public/private key pair as specified in Section 6.3.

   b. TTP generation – The owner obtains the desired assurance when a trusted third party (TTP) who is trusted by the owner generates the public/private key pair as specified in Section 6.3 and provides it to the owner.

2. Key-pair consistency: The owner **shall** perform a pair-wise consistency test by verifying that $m = (m^e)^d \bmod n$ for some integer m satisfying $1 < m < (n-1)$. Note that if the owner generated the key pair (see method 1.a above), an initial pair-wise consistency test was performed during key-pair generation (see Section 6.3). If a TTP generated the key pair and provided it to the owner (see method 1.b above), the owner **shall** perform the consistency check separately, prior to the first use of the key pair in a key-establishment transaction (see Section 4.1).

3. Key-pair validation: A key pair **shall** be validated using one of the following methods:

   a. The owner performs key-pair validation: The owner either

      1) Performs a successful key-pair validation while generating the key pair (see Section 6.3), or

      2) Performs a successful key-pair validation separately from key-pair generation (regardless of whether the owner or a TTP generated the key pair) (see Section 6.4.1.2, 6.4.1.3 or 6.4.1.4).

   b. The TTP performs key-pair validation: A trusted third party (trusted by the owner) either

      1) Performs a successful key-pair validation while generating the key pair (see Section 6.3), or

      2) Performs a successful key-pair validation separately from key-pair generation (as specified in Sections 6.4.1.2, 6.4.1.3 or 6.4.1.4), and indicates the success to the owner. Note that if the key-pair validation is performed separately from the key-pair generation, and the TTP does not have the key pair, then the party that generated the key pair or owns the key pair must provide it to the TTP.

Note that the use of a TTP to generate a key pair or to perform key-pair validation for an owner means that the TTP must be trusted (by both the owner and any recipient) to not use the owner's private key to masquerade as the owner or otherwise compromise the key-establishment transaction.

The key-pair owner can revalidate the key pair at any time using the following steps:

1. Perform a pair-wise consistency test by verifying that $m = (m^e)^d \bmod n$ for some integer m satisfying $1 < m < (n-1)$, and

2, Perform a successful key-pair validation:

a. If the intended value or bit length of the public exponent is known, then perform a successful key-pair validation as specified in Section 6.4.1.2 or 6.4.1.3.

b. If the intended value or bit length of the public exponent is NOT known, then perform a successful key-pair validation as specified in Section 6.4.1.4.

6.4.1.2 RSAKPV1 Family: RSA Key-Pair Validation with a Fixed Public Exponent

The RSAKPV1 family of key-pair validation methods corresponds to the RSAKPG1 family of key-pair generation methods (see Section 6.3.1). RSAKPV1 can be used when the public key, the intended fixed value of the public exponent, the intended bit length of the modulus, the targeted security strength, and the value of the private key are all known by the entity performing the validation.

6.4.1.2.1 *rsakpv1-basic*

rsakpv1-basic is the key-pair validation method corresponding to *rsakpg1-basic* (see Section 6.3.1.1).

Function call: *rsakpv1-basic* (s, $nBits$, e_{fixed}, (n_{pub}, e_{pub}), (n_{priv}, d))

Input:

1. s: the targeted security strength;

2. $nBits$: the intended bit length of the RSA modulus;

3. e_{fixed}: the intended fixed public exponent – an odd integer such that $65{,}537 \leq e_{fixed} < 2^{256}$;

4. (n_{pub}, e_{pub}): the RSA public key to be validated; and

5. (n_{priv}, d): the RSA private key to be validated in the basic format.

Process:

1. Check the sizes of s and e_{fixed}:

    a. If s is not in the interval [112, 256], output an indication that the security strength is not acceptable, and exit without further processing.

    b. If $s > $ ES($nBits$), output an indication that the modulus length is not adequate for the intended security strength, and exit without further processing.

    c. If e_{fixed} is not an odd integer such that $65{,}537 \leq e_{fixed} < 2^{256}$, output an indication that the fixed public exponent is out of range, and exit without further processing.

2. Compare the public exponents:

    If $e_{pub} \neq e_{fixed}$, output an indication of an invalid key pair, and exit without further processing.

3. Check the modulus:

    a. If $n_{pub} \neq n_{priv}$, output an indication of an invalid key pair, and exit without further processing.

    b.   If $\text{len}(n_{pub}) \ne nBits$, output an indication of an invalid key pair, and exit without further processing.

    c.   If *nBits* is not a positive even integer, output an indication of an invalid key pair, and exit without further processing.

4. Prime-factor recovery:

    a.   Recover the prime factors p and q from the modulus n_{pub}, the public exponent e_{pub} and the private exponent d (using one of the methods in <u>Appendix C</u>):

$$(p, q) = \text{RecoverPrimeFactors}\ (n_{pub},\ e_{pub},\ d).$$

    b.   If RecoverPrimeFactors outputs an indication that the prime factors were not found, output an indication that the request is invalid, and exit without further processing.

    c.   If $n_{pub} \ne p \times q$, then output an indication that the request is invalid, and exit without further processing.

5. Check the prime factors:

    a.   If $(p < (\sqrt{2})(2^{nBits/2-1}))$ or $(p > 2^{nBits/2} - 1)$, output an indication of an invalid key pair, and exit without further processing.

    b.   If $(q < (\sqrt{2})(2^{nBits/2-1}))$ or $(q > 2^{nBits/2} - 1)$, output an indication of an invalid key pair, and exit without further processing.

    c.   If $|p - q| \le 2^{(nBits/2-100)}$, output an indication of an invalid key pair, and exit without further processing.

    d.   If $\text{GCD}\ (p - 1, e_{pub}) \ne 1$, output an indication of an invalid key pair, and exit without further processing.

    e.   If $\text{GCD}\ (q - 1, e_{pub}) \ne 1$, output an indication of an invalid key pair, and exit without further processing.

    f.   Apply an **approved** primality test* to the factor p (see <u>FIPS 186</u>, Appendices C.3 and E). If the primality test indicates that p is not prime, output an indication of an invalid key pair, and exit without further processing.

    g.   Apply an **approved** primality test* to the factor q (see <u>FIPS 186</u>, Appendices C.3 and E). If the primality test indicates that q is not prime, output an indication of an invalid key pair, and exit without further processing.

  *   Relying parties (and/or agents trusted to act on their behalf) **shall** determine which of the **approved** primality tests in <u>FIPS 186</u> meet their security requirements. The probability that p or q may be incorrectly classified as prime by the test used in step 5 **shall** be less than or equal to $2^{-\text{ES}(nBits)}$.

6. Check that the private exponent d satisfies

    a. $2^{nBits/2} < d < \text{LCM}\ (p - 1, q - 1)$.

and

b. $1 = (d \times e_{pub}) \bmod \mathrm{LCM}\,(p - 1, q - 1)$.

If either check fails, output an indication of an invalid key pair, and exit without further processing.

7. Output an indication that the key pair is valid.

Output:

1. *status*: An indication that the key pair is valid or an indication of an error.

Errors: Indications of the following:

1. The targeted security strength is not acceptable,

2. The modulus length is not adequate for the targeted security strength,

3. The fixed public exponent is out of range, or

4. The key pair is invalid.

A routine that implements this validation function **shall** destroy any local copies of p, q and d, as well as any other locally stored values used or produced during the execution of the routine. The destruction of these locally stored values **shall** occur prior to or during any exit from the routine (whether exiting early because of an error, or exiting normally).

6.4.1.2.2 *rsakpv1-prime-factor*

rsakpv1-prime-factor is the key-pair validation method corresponding to *rsakpg1-prime-factor* (see Section 6.3.1.2).

Function call: *rsakpv1-prime-factor* $(s, nBits, e_{fixed}, (n_{pub}, e_{pub}), (p, q, d))$

The inputs, outputs and errors are the same as in *rsakpv1-basic* (see Section 6.4.1.2.1) except that the private key is in the prime-factor format: (p, q, d).

The steps are the same as in *rsakpv1-basic* except that in processing:

A. Step 3 is replaced by the following:

3. Check the modulus:

a. If $n_{pub} \neq p \times q$, output an indication of an invalid key pair, and exit without further processing.

b. If len$(n_{pub}) \neq nBits$, output an indication of an invalid key pair, and exit without further processing.

c. If *nBits* is not a positive even integer, output an indication of an invalid key pair, and exit without further processing.

B. Step 4 (prime-factor recovery) is omitted (i.e., not used).

A routine that implements this validation function **shall** destroy any local copies of p, q, and d, as well as any other locally stored values used or produced during the execution of the routine. The destruction of these locally stored values **shall** occur prior to or during any exit from the routine (whether exiting early because of an error, or exiting normally).

6.4.1.2.3   *rsakpv1-crt*

rsakpv1-crt is the key-pair validation method corresponding to *rsakpg1-crt*.

Function call: *rsakpv1-crt* (s, *nBits*, e_{fixed}, (n_{pub}, e_{pub}), (n_{priv}, e_{priv}, d, p, q, dP, dQ, $qInv$))

The inputs, outputs and errors are the same as in *rsakpv1-basic* (see Section 6.4.1.2.1) except that the private key is in the Chinese Remainder Theorem format: (n_{priv}, e_{priv}, d, p, q, dP, dQ, $qInv$).

The steps are the same as in *rsakpv1-basic* except that in processing:

A. Step 2 is replaced by the following:

    2. Compare the public exponents:

        If ($e_{pub} \neq e_{fixed}$) or ($e_{pub} \neq e_{priv}$), output an indication of an invalid key pair, and exit without further processing.

B. Step 3 is replaced by

    3. Check the modulus:

        a. If $n_{pub} \neq p \times q$, or $n_{pub} \neq n_{priv}$, output an indication of an invalid key pair, and exit without further processing.

        b. If len(n_{pub}) $\neq$ *nBits*, output an indication of an invalid key pair, and exit without further processing.

        c. If *nBits* is not a positive even integer, output an indication of an invalid key pair, and exit without further processing.

C. Step 4 (prime-factor recovery) is omitted (i.e., not used),

D. Step 7 is replaced by the following two steps:

    7. Check the CRT components: Check that the components dP, dQ and $qInv$ satisfy

        a. $1 < dP < (p-1)$.

        b. $1 < dQ < (q-1)$.

        c. $1 < qInv < p$.

        d. $1 = (dP \times e_{fixed}) \bmod (p-1)$.

        e. $1 = (dQ \times e_{fixed}) \bmod (q-1)$.

        f. $1 = (qInv \times q) \bmod p$.

        If any of the criteria in Section 6.2.1 are not met, output an indication of an invalid key pair, and exit without further processing.

    8. Output an indication that the key pair is valid.

A routine that implements this validation function **shall** destroy any local copies of p, q, d, dP, dQ, and $qInv$, as well as any other locally stored values used or produced during the execution of the routine. The destruction of these locally stored values **shall** occur prior to or during any exit from the routine (whether exiting early because of an error, or exiting normally).

6.4.1.3 RSAKPV2 Family: RSA Key-Pair Validation (Random Public Exponent)

The RSAKPV2 family of key-pair validation methods corresponds to the RSAKPG2 family of key-pair generation methods (see Section 6.3.2). RSAKPV2 can be used when the public key, the intended bit length of the public exponent, the intended bit length of the modulus, the targeted security strength, and the value of the private key are all known by the entity performing the validation.

6.4.1.3.1 *rsakpv2-basic*

rsakpv2-basic is the validation method corresponding to *rsakpg2-basic* (see Section 6.3.2.1).

Function call: *rsapkv2-basic* (s, $nBits$, $eBits$, (n_{pub}, e_{pub}), (n_{priv}, d))

The method is the same as the *rsapkv1-basic* method in Section 6.4.1.2.1 except that:

A. The e_{fixed} input parameter is replaced by $eBits$, which is the intended bit length of the public exponent – an integer such that $17 \leq eBits \leq 256$.

B. Step 1c is replaced by:

     c. If ($eBits < 17$) or ($eBits > 256$), output an indication that the exponent is out of range, and exit without further processing.

C. Step 2 is replaced by:

     2. Check the public exponent.

         If the public exponent e_{pub} is not odd, or if len(e_{pub}) $\neq$ $eBits$, output an indication of an invalid key pair, and exit without further processing.

A routine that implements this validation function **shall** destroy any local copies of p, q, and d, as well as any other locally stored values used or produced during the execution of the routine. The destruction of these locally stored values **shall** occur prior to or during any exit from the routine (whether exiting early because of an error, or exiting normally).

6.4.1.3.2 *rsakpv2-prime-factor*

rsakpv2-prime-factor is the key-pair validation method corresponding to the *rsakpg2-prime-factor* key-pair generation method (see Section 6.3.2.2).

Function call: *rsakpv2-prime-factor* (s, $nBits$, $eBits$, (n_{pub}, e_{pub}), (p, q, d))

The inputs, outputs and errors are the same as in *rsakpv1-basic* (see Section 6.4.1.2.1), except that the private key is in the prime factor format: (p, q, d).

The steps are the same as in *rsakpv1-basic* (see Section 6.4.1.2.1) except that:

A. The e_{fixed} input parameter is replaced by $eBits$, which is the intended bit length of the public exponent, an integer such that $17 \leq eBits \leq 256$.

B. Step 1c is replaced by:

    c. If ($eBits < 17$) or ($eBits > 256$), output an indication that the exponent is out of range, and exit without further processing.

C. Step 2 is replaced by:

    2. Check the public exponent.

       If the public exponent e_{pub} is not odd, or if len(e_{pub}) $\neq$ $eBits$, output an indication of an invalid key pair, and exit without further processing.

D. Step 3 is replaced by the following:

    3. Check the modulus:

        a. If $n_{pub} \neq p \times q$, output an indication of an invalid key pair, and exit without further processing.

        b. If len(n_{pub}) $\neq$ $nBits$, output an indication of an invalid key pair, and exit without further processing.

        c. If $nBits$ is not a positive even integer, output an indication of an invalid key pair, and exit without further processing.

E. Step 4 (prime-factor recovery) is omitted (i.e., not used).

A routine that implements this validation function **shall** destroy any local copies of p, q, and d, as well as any other locally stored values used or produced during the execution of the routine. The destruction of these locally stored values **shall** occur prior to or during any exit from the routine (whether exiting early because of an error or exiting normally).

6.4.1.3.3 *rsakpv2-crt*

rsakpv2-crt is the key-pair validation method corresponding to the *rsakpg2-crt* key-pair generation method (see Section 6.3.1.3).

Function call: *rsakpv2-crt* (s, $nBits$, $eBits$, (n_{pub}, e_{pub}), (n_{priv}, e_{priv}, d, p, q, dP, dQ, $qInv$))

The inputs, outputs and errors are the same as in *rsakpv1-basic* (see Section 6.4.1.2.1) except that the private key is in the Chinese Remainder Theorem format: (n_{priv}, e_{priv}, d, p, q, dP, dQ, $qInv$).

The steps are the same as in *rsakpv1-basic* (see Section 6.4.1.2.1) except that:

A. The e_{fixed} input parameter is replaced by $eBits$, which is the intended bit length of the public exponent, an integer such that $17 \leq eBits \leq 256$.

B. Step 1c is replaced by:

    c. If ($eBits < 17$) or ($eBits > 256$), output an indication that the exponent is out of range, and exit without further processing.

C. Step 2 is replaced by the following:

    2. Compare the public exponents:

       If ($e_{pub} \neq e_{priv}$) or (e_{pub} is not odd) or (len(e_{pub}) $\neq$ $eBits$), output an indication of an invalid key pair, and exit without further processing.

D. Step 3 is replaced by

   3. Check the modulus:

      a. If $(n_{pub} \neq p \times q)$ or $(n_{pub} \neq n_{priv})$ output an indication of an invalid key pair, and exit without further processing.

      b. If len$(n_{pub}) \neq nBits$, output an indication of an invalid key pair, and exit without further processing.

      c. If $nBits$ is not a positive even integer, output an indication of an invalid key pair, and exit without further processing.

E. Step 4 (prime-factor recovery) is omitted (i.e., not used),

F. Step 7 is replaced by the following two steps:

   7. Check the CRT components: Check that the components dP, dQ and $qInv$ satisfy

      a. $1 < dP < (p-1)$.

      b. $1 < dQ < (q-1)$.

      c. $1 < qInv < p$.

      d. $1 = (dP \times e_{pub}) \bmod (p-1)$.

      e. $1 = (dQ \times e_{pub}) \bmod (q-1)$.

      f. $1 = (qInv \times q) \bmod p$.

If any of the criteria in Section 6.2.1 are not met, output an indication of an invalid key pair, and exit without further processing.

   8. Output an indication that the key pair is valid.

A routine that implements this validation function **shall** destroy any local copies of p, q, d, dP, dQ, and $qInv$, as well as any other locally stored values used or produced during the execution of the routine. The destruction of these locally stored values **shall** occur prior to or during any exit from the routine (whether exiting early because of an error, or exiting normally).

6.4.1.4 RSA Key-Pair Validation (Exponent-Creation Method Unknown)

Public-key validation may be performed when the intended fixed value or intended bit length of the public exponent is unknown by the entity performing the validation (i.e., the entity is unaware of whether the key pair was generated as specified in Section 6.3.1 or Section 6.3.2). The following methods can be used as long as the entity performing the validation (i.e., the key-pair owner or a TTP trusted by the owner) knows the intended bit length of the modulus and the targeted security strength, and has possession of some representation of the key pair to be validated (including the private key in either the *basic*, *prime factor* or *crt* format).

6.4.1.4.1 *basic-pkv*

In this format, the private key is represented as (n, d).

Function call: *basic_pkv* $(s, nBits, (n_{pub}, e_{pub}), (n_{priv}, d))$

The method is the same as the *rsapkv1-basic* method in Section 6.4.1.2.1 except that:

A. A value for e_{fixed} is not available as an input parameter.

B. Step 1.c is replaced by:

> If e_{pub} is not an odd integer such that $65{,}537 \le e_{pub} < 2^{256}$, output an indication that the exponent is out of range, and exit without further processing.

C. Step 2 is omitted (i.e., not used).

A routine that implements this validation function **shall** destroy any local copies of p, q, and d, as well as any other locally stored values used or produced during the execution of the routine. The destruction of these locally stored values **shall** occur prior to or during any exit from the routine (whether exiting early because of an error or exiting normally).

6.4.1.4.2 *prime-factor-pkv*

In this format, the private key is represented as (p, q, d).

Function call: *prime-factor_pkv* $(s, nBits, (n_{pub}, e_{pub}), (p, q, d))$

The inputs, outputs and errors are the same as in *rsakpv1-basic* (see Section 6.4.1.2.1) except that the private key is in the prime factor format: (p, q, d).

The steps are the same as in *rsakpv1-basic* (see Section 6.4.1.2.1) except that:

A. A value for e_{fixed} is not available as an input parameter.

B. Step 1.c is replaced by:

> If e_{pub} is not an odd integer such that $65{,}537 \le e_{pub} < 2^{256}$, output an indication that the exponent is out of range, and exit without further processing.

C. Step 2 is omitted (i.e., not used).

D. Step 3 is replaced by the following:

> 3. Check the modulus:
>
>> a. If $n_{pub} \ne p \times q$, output an indication of an invalid key pair, and exit without further processing.
>>
>> b. If $len(n_{pub}) \ne nBits$, output an indication of an invalid key pair, and exit without further processing.
>>
>> c. If $nBits$ is not a positive even integer, output an indication of an invalid key pair, and exit without further processing.

E. Step 4 (prime-factor recovery) is omitted (i.e., not used).

A routine that implements this validation function **shall** destroy any local copies of p, q, and d, as well as any other locally stored values used or produced during its the execution of the routine. Their destruction of these values **shall** occur prior to or during any exit from the routine (whether exiting early because of an error, or exiting normally).

6.4.1.4.3 crt_pkv

In this format, the private key is represented as $(n, e, d, p, q, dP, dQ, qInv)$.

Function call: $crt\_pkv(s, nBits, (n_{pub}, e_{pub}), (n_{priv}, e_{priv}, d, p, q, dP, dQ, qInv))$

The inputs, outputs and errors are the same as in *rsakpv1-basic* (see Section 6.4.1.2.1) except that the private key is in the Chinese Remainder Theorem (CRT) format: $(n_{priv}, e_{priv}, d, p, q, dP, dQ, qInv)$.

The steps are the same as in *rsakpv1-basic* (see Section 6.4.1.2.1) except that:

A. A value for e_{fixed} is not available as an input parameter.

B. Step 1c is replaced by:

> If e_{pub} is not an odd integer such that $65{,}537 \le e_{pub} < 2^{256}$, output an indication that the exponent is out of range, and exit without further processing.

C. Step 2 is omitted (i.e., not used).

D. Step 3 is replaced by

> 3. Check the modulus:
>
>   a. If $(n_{pub} \ne p \times q)$ or $(n_{pub} \ne n_{priv})$, output an indication of an invalid key pair, and exit without further processing.
>
>   b. If $len(n_{pub}) \ne nBits$, output an indication of an invalid key pair, and exit without further processing.
>
>   c. If *nBits* is not a positive even integer, output an indication of an invalid key pair, and exit without further processing.

E. Step 4 (prime-factor recovery) is omitted (i.e., not used),

F. Step 7 is replaced by the following two steps:

> 7. Check the CRT components: Check that the components dP, dQ and $qInv$ satisfy
>
>   a. $1 < dP < (p-1)$.
>
>   b. $1 < dQ < (q-1)$.
>
>   c. $1 < qInv < p$.
>
>   d. $1 = (dP \times e_{pub}) \bmod (p-1)$.
>
>   e. $1 = (dQ \times e_{pub}) \bmod (q-1)$.
>
>   f. $1 = (qInv \times q) \bmod p$.
>
>   If any of the criteria in Section 6.2.1 are not met, output an indication of an invalid key pair, and exit without further processing.
>
> 8. Output an indication that the key pair is valid.

A routine that implements this validation function **shall** destroy any local copies of p, q, dP, dQ, and $qInv$, as well as any other locally stored values used or produced during the execution of the routine. The destruction of these locally stored values **shall** occur prior to or during any exit from the routine (whether exiting early because of an error or exiting normally).

6.4.1.5 Owner Assurance of Private-Key Possession

An owner's initial assurance of possession of his private key is obtained when assurance of key-pair validity is obtained (see Section 6.4.1.1); assurance of key-pair validity is required prior to the owner's use of a key pair for key establishment. As time passes, an owner could lose possession of the private key of a key pair. For this reason, renewing the assurance of possession may be appropriate for some applications (i.e., assurance of possession can be refreshed). A discussion of the effect of time on the assurance of private-key possession is provided in SP 800-89.

When renewed assurance that the owner continues to possess the correct associated private key is required, it **shall** be obtained in one or more of the following ways:

1. The key-pair owner renews assurance of key-pair validity – The owner obtains assurance of renewed key-pair validity as specified in Section 6.4.1.1, thereby also obtaining renewed assurance of private key possession.

2. The key-pair owner receives renewed assurance via key confirmation – The owner employs the key pair to successfully engage a trusted second party in a key-agreement transaction using a scheme from the **KAS2** family that incorporates key confirmation. The key confirmation **shall** be performed in order to obtain assurance that the private key(s) function correctly.

    -   The **KAS2-Party_V-confirmation** scheme in Section 8.3.3.2 can be used to provide assurance to a key-pair owner, acting as party U, that both parties are in possession of the correct private key; i.e., when the key confirmation is successful, party U obtains assurance that party V possesses the private key corresponding to $PubKey_V$, and that party U possesses the private key corresponding to $PubKey_U$, where $PubKey_V$ and $PubKey_U$ are the public keys associated with parties V and U, respectively, that were used during that **KAS2-Party_V-confirmation** transaction.

    -   The **KAS2-Party_U-confirmation** scheme in Section 8.3.3.3 can be used to provide assurance to a key-pair owner, acting as party V, that both parties are in possession of the correct private key; i.e., when the key confirmation is successful, party V has obtained assurance that party U possesses the private key corresponding to $PubKey_U$ and that party V possesses the private key corresponding to $PubKey_V$, where $PubKey_U$ and $PubKey_V$ are the public keys associated with parties U and V, respectively, that were used during that **KAS2-Party_U-confirmation** transaction.

    -   The **KAS2-bilateral-confirmation** scheme in Section 8.3.3.4 can be used to provide assurance to a key-pair owner acting as either party U or party V that both parties are in possession of the correct private key; i.e., when the bilateral key-confirmation is successful, each party has obtained assurance that party U possesses the private key corresponding to $PubKey_U$, and that party V possesses the private key corresponding to $PubKey_V$, where $PubKey_U$ and $PubKey_V$ are the public keys associated with parties U and V, respectively, that were used during that **KAS2-bilateral-confirmation** transaction."

3. The owner receives assurance via an encrypted certificate - The key-pair owner uses the private key while engaging in a key-establishment transaction with a Certificate Authority (trusted by the owner) using a scheme in this Recommendation after providing the CA with the corresponding public key. As part of this transaction, the CA generates a (new) certificate containing the owner's public key and encrypts that certificate using (some portion of) the symmetric keying material that has been established. Only the encrypted form of the certificate is provided to the owner. By successfully decrypting the certificate and verifying the CA's signature, the owner obtains assurance of possession of the correct private key (at the time of the key-establishment transaction).

The key-pair owner (or agents trusted to act on the owner's behalf) **should** determine that the method used for obtaining renewed assurance of the owner's possession of the correct private key is sufficient and appropriate to meet the security requirements of the owner's intended application(s).

6.4.2 Assurances Required by a Public-Key Recipient

In this Recommendation, unless otherwise indicated, a recipient of the public key of another party is assumed to be an entity that does not have (and is not authorized to have) access to the corresponding private key. The recipient of the (purported) public key-establishment key of another party **shall** have:

1. Assurance of the arithmetic validity of the other party's public key before using it in a key-establishment transaction with its claimed owner, and (if used)

2. Assurance that the claimed public-key owner (i.e., the other party) actually possesses the private key corresponding to that public key.

6.4.2.1 Obtaining Assurance of Public-Key Validity for a Received Public Key

The recipient **shall** obtain assurance of public-key validity using one or more of the following methods:

1. Recipient Partial Public-Key Validation – The recipient performs a successful partial public-key validation (see Section 6.4.2.2).

2. TTP Partial Public-Key Validation – The recipient receives assurance that a trusted third party (trusted by the recipient) has performed a successful partial public-key validation (see Section 6.4.2.2).

3. TTP Key-Pair Validation – The recipient receives assurance that a trusted third party (trusted by the recipient and the owner) has performed key-pair validation in accordance with Section 6.4.1.1 (step 3.b).

   Note that the use of a TTP to perform key-pair validation (method 3) implies that both the owner and any recipient of the public key trust that the TTP will not use the owner's private key to masquerade as the owner or otherwise compromise their key-establishment transactions.

6.4.2.2 Partial Public-Key Validation for RSA

Partial public-key validation for RSA consists of conducting plausibility tests. These tests determine whether the public modulus and public exponent are plausible, not necessarily whether they are completely valid, i.e., they may not conform to all RSA key-generation requirements as specified in this Recommendation. Plausibility tests can detect unintentional errors with a reasonable probability. Note that full RSA public-key validation is not specified in this Recommendation, as it is an area of ongoing research. Therefore, if an application requires assurance of full public-key validation, then another **approved** key-establishment method **shall** be used (e.g., as specified in SP 800-56A).

Plausibility tests **shall** include the tests specified in Section 5.3.3 of SP 800-89, with the caveat that the bit length of the modulus **shall** be a length that is **approved** in this Recommendation.

6.4.2.3 Recipient Assurances of an Owner's Possession of a Private Key

When two parties engage in a key-establishment transaction, there is (at least) an implicit claim of ownership made whenever a public key is provided on behalf of a particular party. That party is considered to be a *claimed* owner of the corresponding key pair – as opposed to being a *true* owner – until adequate assurance can be provided that the party is actually the one authorized to use the private key. The claimed owner can provide such assurance by demonstrating its knowledge of that private key.

The recipient of another party's public key **shall** obtain an initial assurance that the other party (i.e., the claimed owner of the public key) actually possesses the associated private key, either prior to or concurrently with performing a key-establishment transaction with that other party. Obtaining this assurance is addressed in Sections 6.4.2.3.1 and 6.4.2.3.2. As time passes, renewing the assurance of possession may be appropriate for some applications; assurance of possession can be renewed as specified in Section 6.4.2.3.2. A discussion of the effect of time on the assurance of private-key possession is provided in SP 800-89.

As part of the proper implementation of this Recommendation, system users and/or agents trusted to act on their behalf **should** determine which of the methods for obtaining assurance of possession meet their security requirements. The application tasked with performing key establishment on behalf of a party **should** determine whether or not to proceed with a key-establishment transaction, based upon the perceived adequacy of the method(s) used. Such knowledge may be explicitly provided to the application in some manner, or may be implicitly provided by the operation of the application itself.

If a binding authority is the public-key recipient: At the time of binding an owner's identifier to his public key, the binding authority (i.e., a trusted third party, such as a CA) **shall** obtain assurance that the owner is in possession of the correct private key. This assurance **shall** either be obtained using one of the methods specified in Section 6.4.2.3.2 (e.g., with the binding authority acting as the public-key recipient) or by using an **approved** alternative (see SP 800-57, Part 1, Sections 5.2 and 8.1.5.1.1.2).

Recipients not acting in the role of a binding authority: The recipients **shall** obtain this assurance either through a trusted third party (see Section 6.4.2.3.1) or directly from the owner (i.e., the other party) (see Section 6.4.2.3.2) before using the derived keying material for purposes beyond those required during the key-establishment transaction itself. If the recipient chooses to obtain this assurance directly from the other party (i.e., the claimed owner of that public key), then to comply with this Recommendation, the recipient **shall** use one of the methods specified in Section 6.4.2.3.2.

Note that the requirement that assurance of possession be obtained before using the established keying material for purposes *beyond* those of the key-establishment transaction itself does not prohibit the parties to a key-establishment transaction from using a portion of the derived or transported keying material *during* the key-establishment transaction for purposes required by that key-establishment scheme. For example, in a transaction involving a key-agreement scheme that incorporates key confirmation, the parties establish a (purported) shared secret, derive keying material, and – as part of that same transaction – use a portion of the derived keying material as the MAC key in their key-confirmation computations.

6.4.2.3.1 Recipient Obtains Assurance from a Trusted Third Party

The recipient of a public key may receive assurance that its owner (i.e., the other party in the key-establishment transaction) is in possession of the correct private key from a trusted third party (trusted by the recipient), either before or during a key-establishment transaction that makes use of that public key. The methods used by a third party trusted by the recipient to obtain that assurance are beyond the scope of this Recommendation (see however, the discussions in Sections 6.4.2.3.2 below and in 8.1.5.1.1.2 of SP 800-57).

The recipient of a public key (or agents trusted to act on behalf of the recipient) **should** know the method(s) used by the third party, in order to determine that the assurance obtained on behalf of the recipient is sufficient and appropriate to meet the security requirements of the recipient's intended application(s).

6.4.2.3.2 Recipient Obtains Assurance Directly from the Claimed Owner (i.e., the Other Party)

The recipient of a public key can directly obtain assurance of the claimed owner's current possession of the corresponding private key by successfully completing a key-establishment transaction that explicitly incorporates key confirmation, with the claimed owner serving as the key-confirmation provider. Note that the recipient of the public key in question will also be the key-confirmation recipient. Also note that this use of key confirmation is an additional benefit beyond its use to confirm that two parties possess the same keying material.

There are several key-establishment schemes specified in this Recommendation that can be used. In order to claim conformance with this Recommendation, the key-establishment transaction during which the recipient of a public key seeks to obtain assurance of its owner's current possession of the corresponding private key **shall** employ one of the following **approved** key-establishment schemes:

1. The **KAS1-Party_V-confirmation** scheme in Section 8.2.3.2 can be used to provide assurance to party U that party V possesses the private key corresponding to $PubKey_V$, (the public key that was associated with party V when that key pair is used during the key-agreement transaction).

2. The **KAS2-Party_V-confirmation** scheme in Section 8.3.3.2 can be used to provide assurance to party U that party V possesses the private key corresponding to *PubKey_V* (the public key that was associated with party V when that key pair is used during the key-agreement transaction).

3. The **KAS2-Party_U-confirmation** scheme in Section 8.3.3.3 can be used to provide assurance to party V that party U possesses the private key corresponding to *PubKey_U* (the public key that was associated with party U when that key pair is used during the key-agreement transaction).

4. The **KAS2-bilateral-confirmation** scheme in Section 8.3.3.4 can be used to provide assurance to each party that the other party possesses the correct private key that corresponds to the other party's public key; i.e., when bilateral key-confirmation is successful, party U obtains assurance that party V possesses the private key corresponding to *PubKey_V* (the key pair that was associated with party V and that was used during the key-agreement transaction), and party V obtains assurance that party U possesses the private key corresponding to *PubKey_U* (the key pair that was associated with party U and that was used during the key-agreement transaction).

5. The **KTS-OAEP-Party_V-confirmation** scheme in Section 9.2.4.2 can be used to provide assurance to party U (the key-transport sender) that party V (the key-transport receiver) possesses the private key corresponding to *PubKey_V* (the key pair that was associated with party V and that was used during the key-agreement transaction).

The recipient of a public key (or agents trusted to act on the recipient's behalf) **shall** determine whether or not using one of the key-establishment schemes in this Recommendation to obtain assurance of possession through key confirmation is sufficient and appropriate to meet the security requirements of the recipient's intended application(s). Other **approved** methods (e.g., see Section 5.4.4 of SP 800-57-Part 1) of directly obtaining this assurance of possession from the owner are also allowed. If obtaining assurance of possession directly from the owner is not acceptable, then assurance of possession **shall** be obtained indirectly as discussed in Section 6.4.2.3.1.

Successful key confirmation (performed in the context described in this Recommendation) demonstrates that the correct private key has been used in the key-confirmation provider's calculations, and thus also provides assurance that the claimed owner is the true owner.

The assurance of possession obtained via the key-confirmation schemes identified above may be useful even when the recipient has previously obtained independent assurance that the claimed owner of a public key is indeed its true owner. This may be appropriate in situations where the recipient desires renewed assurance that the owner possesses the correct private key (and that the owner is still able to use it correctly), including situations where there is no access to a trusted party who can provide renewed assurance of the owner's continued possession of the private key.

7   Primitives and Operations

Except for RSADP (see Section 7.1.2), the primitives and operations are defined in this section as if the RSA private keys are in the basic format. Equivalent primitives and operations that employ RSA private keys given in the prime-factor or CRT format are permitted (see Section 7.1.2.3).

7.1   Encryption and Decryption Primitives

RSAEP and RSADP are the basic encryption and decryption primitives from the RSA cryptosystem [RSA 1978] specified in PKCS 1. RSAEP produces ciphertext from plaintext using a public key; RSADP recovers the plaintext from the ciphertext using the corresponding private key. The primitives assume that the RSA public key is valid.

7.1.1   RSAEP

RSAEP produces ciphertext using an RSA public key.

Function call: RSAEP($(n, e), m$)

Input:

1. (n, e): the RSA public key.

2. m: the plaintext; an integer such that $1 < m < (n - 1)$.

Assumption: The RSA public key is valid (see Section 6.4).

Process:

1. If m does not satisfy $1 < m < (n - 1)$, output an indication that m is out of range, and exit without further processing.

2. Let $c = m^e \bmod n$.

3. Output c.

Output:

   c: the ciphertext, an integer such that $1 < c < (n - 1)$, or an error indicator.

A routine that implements this primitive **shall** destroy any local copies of the input m, as well as any other potentially sensitive locally stored values used or produced during the execution of the routine. The destruction of these values **shall** occur prior to or during any exit from the routine (whether exiting early because of an error or exiting normally with the output of c).

7.1.2   RSADP

RSADP is the decryption primitive. It recovers the plaintext from ciphertext using an RSA private key. The format of the decryption operation depends on the format of the private key: basic, prime factor or CRT.

A routine that implements this primitive **shall** destroy any local copies of the private key, as well as any other potentially sensitive locally stored values used or produced during the execution of the routine (such as any locally stored portions of the plaintext). The destruction of these values

shall occur prior to or during any exit from the routine (whether exiting early because of an error or exiting normally, with the output of plaintext).

Note:

> Care **should** be taken to ensure that an implementation of RSADP does not reveal even partial information about the value of the plaintext to unauthorized entities. An opponent who can reliably obtain particular bits of the plaintext for sufficiently many chosen ciphertext values may be able to obtain the full decryption of an arbitrary ciphertext by applying the bit-security results of Håstad and Näslund [HN 1998].

7.1.2.1 Decryption with the Private Key in the Basic Format

Function call: RSADP$((n, d), c)$

Input:

1. (n, d): the RSA private key.

2. c: the ciphertext; an integer such that $1 < c < (n - 1)$.

Process:

1. If the ciphertext c does not satisfy $1 < c < (n - 1)$, output an indication that the ciphertext is out of range, and exit without further processing.

2. Let $m = c^d \bmod n$.

3. Output m.

Output:

> m: the plaintext; an integer such that $1 < m < (n - 1)$, or an error indicator.

7.1.2.2 Decryption with the Private Key in the Prime Factor Format

Function call: RSADP$((p, q, d), c)$

Input:

1. (p, q, d): the RSA private key.

2. c: the ciphertext; an integer such that $1 < c < (n - 1)$.

Process:

1. If the ciphertext c does not satisfy $1 < c < (n - 1)$, output an indication that the ciphertext is out of range, and exit without further processing.

2. Let $n = p \times q$, the product of p and q.

3. Let $m = c^d \bmod n$.

4. Output m.

Output:

m: the plaintext; an integer such that $1 < m < (n - 1)$, or an error indicator.

7.1.2.3 Decryption with the Private Key in the CRT Format

Function call: RSADP($n, e, d, p, q, dP, dQ, qInv, c$)

1. ($n, e, d, p, q, dP, dQ, qInv$): the RSA private key, where $dP = d \bmod (p - 1)$, $dQ = d \bmod (q - 1)$ and $qInv = q \bmod p$.

2. *c*: the ciphertext; an integer such that $1 < c < (n - 1)$.

Process:

1. If the ciphertext *c* does not satisfy $1 < c < (n - 1)$, output an indication that the ciphertext is out of range, and exit without further processing.

2. $m_p = c^{dP} \bmod p$.

3. $m_q = c^{dQ} \bmod q$.

4. Let $h = ((m_p - m_q) \times qInv) \bmod p$.

5. Let $m = (m_q + (q \times h)) \bmod n$.

6. Output *m*.

7.2 Encryption and Decryption Operations

7.2.1 RSA Secret-Value Encapsulation (RSASVE)

The RSASVE generate operation is used by one party in a key-establishment transaction to generate and encrypt a secret value to produce ciphertext using the public key-establishment key of the other party. When this ciphertext is received by that other party, and the secret value is recovered (using the RSASVE recover operation and the corresponding private key-establishment key), the secret value is then considered to be a shared secret. Secret-value encapsulation employs a Random Bit Generator (RBG) to generate the secret value.

The RSASVE generate and recovery operations specified in Sections 7.2.1.2 and 7.2.1.3, respectively, are based on the RSAEP and RSADP primitives (see Section 7.1). These operations are used by the **KAS1** and **KAS2** key-agreement families (see Sections 8.2 and 8.3).

7.2.1.1 RSASVE Components

RSASVE uses the following components:

1. RBG: An **approved** random bit generator (see Section 5.3).

2. RSAEP: RSA Encryption Primitive (see Section 7.1.1).

3. RSADP: RSA Decryption Primitive (see Section 7.1.2).

7.2.1.2 RSASVE Generate Operation (RSASVE.GENERATE)

RSASVE.GENERATE generates a secret value and corresponding ciphertext using an RSA public key.

Function call: **RSASVE.GENERATE**$((n, e))$

Input:

> (n, e): an RSA public key.

Assumptions: The RSA public key is valid.

Process:

1. Compute the value of $nLen = \lceil \operatorname{len}(n)/8 \rceil$, the byte length of the modulus n.

2. Generation:

   a. Using the RBG (see Section 5.3), generate Z, a byte string of $nLen$ bytes.

   b. Convert Z to an integer z (See Appendix B.2):

   $$z = \text{BS2I}(Z, nLen).$$

   c. If z does not satisfy $1 < z < (n - 1)$, then go to step 2a.

3. RSA encryption:

   a. Apply the RSAEP encryption primitive (see Section 7.1.1) to the integer z using the public key (n, e) to produce an integer ciphertext c:

   $$c = \text{RSAEP}((n, e), z).$$

   b. Convert the ciphertext c to a ciphertext byte string C of $nLen$ bytes (see Appendix B.1):

   $$C = \text{I2BS}(c, nLen).$$

4. Output the string Z as the secret value, and the ciphertext C.

Output:

> Z: the secret value to be shared (a byte string of $nLen$ bytes), and C: the ciphertext (a byte string of $nLen$ bytes).

A routine that implements this operation **shall** destroy any locally stored portions of Z and z, as well as any other potentially sensitive locally stored values used or produced during the execution of the routine. The destruction of these values **shall** occur prior to or during any exit from the routine (whether exiting early because of an error or exiting normally with the output of Z and C). Note that the requirement for destruction includes any locally stored portions of the secret value Z included in the output.

7.2.1.3 RSASVE Recovery Operation (RSASVE.RECOVER)

RSASVE.RECOVER recovers a secret value from ciphertext using an RSA private key. Once recovered, the secret value is considered to be a shared secret.

Function call:

RSASVE.RECOVER$((n, d), C)$

Input:

1. (n, d): an RSA private key.

2. C: the ciphertext; a byte string of $nLen$ bytes.

Assumptions: The RSA private key is part of a valid key pair.

Process:

1. $nLen = \lceil \operatorname{len}(n)/8 \rceil$, the byte length of n.

2. Length checking:

   If the length of the ciphertext C is not $nLen$ bytes in length, output an indication of a decryption error, and exit without further processing.

3. RSA decryption:

   a. Convert the ciphertext C to an integer ciphertext c (see Appendix B.2):

   $$c = \operatorname{BS2I}(C).$$

   b. Apply the RSADP decryption primitive (see Section 7.1.2) to the ciphertext c using the private key (n, d) to produce an integer z:

   $$z = \operatorname{RSADP}((n, d), c).[23]$$

   c. If RSADP indicates that the ciphertext is out of range, output an indication of a decryption error, and exit without further processing.

   d. Convert the integer z to a byte string Z of $nLen$ bytes (see Appendix B.1):

   $$Z = \operatorname{I2BS}(z, nLen).$$

4. Output the string Z as the secret value (i.e., the shared secret), or an error indicator.

Output:

Z: the secret value/shared secret (a byte string of $nLen$ bytes), or an error indicator.

Note:

Care **should** be taken to ensure that an implementation does not reveal information about the encapsulated secret value (i.e., the value of the integer z or its byte string equivalent Z). For instance, the observable behavior of the I2BS routine **should not** reveal even partial

---

[23] When the private key is represented in the prime-factor or CRT format, appropriate changes are discussed in Section 7.1.2.

information about the byte string Z. An opponent who can reliably obtain particular bits of Z for sufficiently many chosen ciphertext values may be able to obtain the full decryption of an arbitrary RSA-encrypted value by applying the bit-security results of Håstad and Näslund [HN 1998].

A routine that implements this operation **shall** destroy any local copies of the private key, any locally stored portions of Z and z, and any other potentially sensitive locally stored values used or produced during the execution of this routine. The destruction of these locally stored values **shall** occur prior to or during any exit from the routine (whether exiting early because of an error or exiting normally with the output of Z). Note that the requirement for destruction includes any locally stored portions of the output.

7.2.2 RSA with Optimal Asymmetric Encryption Padding (RSA-OAEP)

RSA-OAEP consists of asymmetric encryption and decryption operations that are based on an **approved** hash function, an **approved** random bit generator, a mask-generation function, and the RSAEP and RSADP primitives. These operations are used by the **KTS-OAEP** key-transport scheme (see Section 9.2).

In the RSA-OAEP encryption operation, a data block is constructed by the sender (party U) from the keying material to be transported and the hash of additional input (see Section 9.1) that is shared by party U and the intended receiving party (party V). A random byte string is generated, after which both the random byte string and the data block are masked in a way that binds their values. The masked values are used to form the plaintext that is input to the RSAEP primitive, along with the public key-establishment key of party V. The resulting RSAEP output further binds the random byte string, the keying material and the hash of the additional data in the ciphertext that is sent to party V.

In the RSA-OAEP decryption operation, the ciphertext and the receiving party's (i.e., party V's) private key-establishment key are input to the RSADP primitive, recovering the masked values as output. The mask-generation function is then used to reconstruct and remove the masks that obscure the random byte string and the data block. After removing the masks, party V can examine the format of the recovered data and compare its own computation of the hash of the additional data to the hash value contained in the unmasked data block, thus obtaining some measure of assurance of the integrity of the recovered data – including the transported keying material.

RSA-OAEP can process up to $nLen - 2HLen - 2$ bytes of keying material, where $nLen$ is the byte length of the recipient's RSA modulus, and $HLen$ is the byte length of the values output by the underlying hash function.

7.2.2.1 RSA-OAEP Components

RSA-OAEP uses the following components:

1. H: An **approved** hash function (see Section 5.1). $HLen$ is used to denote the byte length of the hash function output.

2. MGF: The mask-generation function (see Section 7.2.2.2). The MGF employs a hash function *hash*. This hash function need not be the same as the hash function H used in step 3a of Section 7.2.2.3 and step 4a of Section 7.2.2.4.

3. RBG: An **approved** random bit generator (see Section 5.3).

4. RSAEP: RSA Encryption Primitive (see Section 7.1.1).

5. RSADP: RSA Decryption Primitive (see Section 7.1.2).

7.2.2.2 The Mask Generation Function (MGF)

MGF is a mask-generation function based on an **approved** hash function (see Section 5.1). The purpose of the MGF is to generate a string of bits that may be used to "mask" other bit strings. The MGF is used by the RSA-OAEP-based schemes specified in Section 9.2.

Let *hash* be an **approved** hash function.

For the purposes of this Recommendation, the MGF **shall not** be invoked more than once by each party during a given transaction using a given MGF seed (i.e., a mask **shall** be derived only once by each party from a given MGF seed).

Function call: MGF(*mgfSeed*, *maskLen*)

Auxiliary Function:

    hash: an **approved** hash function (see Section 5.1).

Implementation-Dependent Parameters:

1. *hashLen*: an integer that indicates the byte length of the output block of the auxiliary hash function, *hash*.

2. *max_hash_inputLen*: an integer that indicates the maximum-permitted byte length of the bit string, *x*, that is used as input to the auxiliary hash function, *hash*.

Input:

1. *mgfSeed*: a byte string from which the mask is generated.

2. *maskLen*: the intended byte length of the mask.

Process:

1. If *maskLen* > 2^{32} *hashLen*, output an error indicator, and exit from this process without performing the remaining actions.

2. If *mgfSeed* is more than *max_hash_inputLen* bytes in length, then output an error indicator, and exit this process without performing the remaining actions.

3. Set *T* = the null string.

4. For *counter* from 0 to $\lceil maskLen / hashLen \rceil - 1$, do the following:

    a) Let *D* = I2BS(*counter*, 4)   (see Appendix B.1).

    b) Let *T* = *T* || *hash*(*mgfSeed* || *D*).

5. Output the leftmost *maskLen* bytes of *T* as the byte string *mask*.

Output:

The byte string *mask* (of *maskLen* bytes), or an error indicator.

A routine that implements this function **shall** destroy any local copies of the input *mgfSeed*, any locally stored portions of *mask* (e.g., any portion of *T*), and any other potentially sensitive locally stored values used or produced during the execution of the routine. The destruction of these locally stored values **shall** occur prior to or during any exit from the routine (whether exiting early because of an error or exiting normally with the output of *mask*). Note that the requirement for destruction includes any locally stored portions of the output.

7.2.2.3 RSA-OAEP Encryption Operation (RSA-OAEP.ENCRYPT)

The RSA-OAEP.ENCRYPT operation produces ciphertext from keying material and additional input using an RSA public key, as shown in Figure 4. See Section 9.1 for more information on the additional input. Let *HLen* be the byte length of the output of hash function H.

Function call: RSA-OAEP.ENCRYPT$((n, e), K, A)$

Input*:*

1. (n, e): the receiver's RSA public key.

2. *K*: the keying material; a byte string of at most *nLen* − 2*HLen* − 2 bytes, where *nlen* is the byte length of *n*.

3. *A*: additional input; a byte string (which may be the *Null* string) to be cryptographically bound to the keying material (see Section 9.1).

Assumptions: The RSA public key is valid.

Process*:*

1. $nLen = \lceil \operatorname{len}(n)/8 \rceil$, the byte length of *n*.

2. Length checking:

    a. $KLen = \lceil \operatorname{len}(K)/8 \rceil$, the byte length of *K*.

    b. If *KLen* > *nLen* − 2*HLen* − 2, then output an indication that the keying material is too long, and exit without further processing.

3. OAEP encoding:

    a. Apply the selected hash function to compute:

    $$HA = \mathrm{H}(A).$$

    HA is a byte string of *HLen* bytes. If *A* is an empty string, then *HA* is the hash value for the empty string.

    b. Construct a byte string *PS* consisting of *nLen* − *KLen* − 2*HLen* − 2 zero bytes. The length of *PS* may be zero.

    c. Concatenate *HA*, *PS*, a single byte with a hexadecimal value of 01, and the keying material *K* to form data *DB* of *nLen* − *HLen* − 1 bytes as follows:

$$DB = HA \parallel PS \parallel 00000001 \parallel K,$$

where 00000001 is a string of eight bits.

d. Using the RBG (see Section 5.3), generate a random byte string *mgfSeed* of *HLen* bytes.

e. Apply the mask-generation function in Section 7.2.2.2 to compute:

$$dbMask = \text{MGF}(mgfSeed, nLen - HLen - 1).$$

f. Let *maskedDB* = *DB* ⊕ *dbMask*.

g. Apply the mask-generation function in Section 7.2.2.2 to compute:

$$mgfSeedMask = \text{MGF}(maskedDB, HLen).$$

h. Let *maskedMGFSeed* = *mgfSeed* ⊕ *mgfSeedMask*.

i. Concatenate a single byte with hexadecimal value 00, *maskedMGFSeed*, and *maskedDB* to form an encoded message *EM* of *nLen* bytes as follows:

$$EM = 00000000 \parallel maskedMGFSeed \parallel maskedDB,$$

where 00000000 is a sting of eight bits.

4. RSA encryption:

a. Convert the encoded message *EM* to an integer *em* (see Appendix B.2):

$$em = \text{BS2I}(EM).$$

b. Apply RSAEP (see Section 7.1.1) to the integer *em* using the public key (*n*, *e*) to produce a ciphertext integer *c*:

$$c = \text{RSAEP}((n, e), em).$$

c. Convert the ciphertext integer *c* to a ciphertext byte string *C* of *nLen* bytes (see Appendix B.1):

$$C = \text{I2BS}(c, nLen).$$

5. Zeroize all intermediate values and output the ciphertext *C*.

Output: C: the ciphertext (a byte string of *nLen* bytes), or an error indicator.

A routine that implements this operation **shall** destroy any local copies of sensitive input values (e.g., *K* and any sensitive portions of *A*), as well as any other potentially sensitive locally stored values used or produced during the execution of the routine (including *HA, DB, mfgSeed, dbMask, maskedDB, mgfSeedMask, maskedMGFSeed, EM,* and *em*). The destruction of these locally stored values **shall** occur prior to or during any exit from the routine – whether exiting early because of an error or exiting normally with the output of *C*.

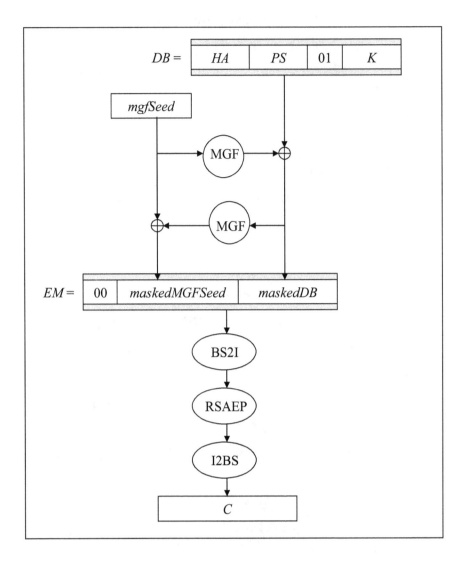

Figure 4: RSA-OAEP Encryption Operation

7.2.2.4 RSA-OAEP Decryption Operation (RSA-OAEP.DECRYPT)

RSA-OAEP.DECRYPT recovers keying material from a ciphertext string and additional input using an RSA private key as shown in Figure 5. Let *HLen* be the byte length of the output of hash function H.

Function call: RSA-OAEP.DECRYPT$((n, d), C, A)$

Input:

1. (n, d): the receiver's RSA private key.

2. C: the ciphertext; a byte string.

3. A: additional input; a byte string (which may be the empty string) whose cryptographic binding to the keying material is to be verified (see Section 9.1).

Assumptions: The RSA private key is valid.

Process:

1. Initializations:

    a. *nLen* = the byte length of *n*. For this Recommendation, $nLen \geq 256$.

    b. *DecryptErrorFlag = False*.

2. Check for erroneous input:

    a. If the length of the ciphertext *C* is not *nLen* bytes, output an indication of erroneous input, and exit without further processing.

    b. Convert the ciphertext byte string *C* to a ciphertext integer *c* (see Appendix B.2):

    $$c = \text{BS2I}(C).$$

    c. If the ciphertext integer *c* is not such that $1 < c < (n - 1)$, output an indication of erroneous input, and exit without further processing.

3. RSA decryption:

    a. Apply RSADP (see Section 7.1.2) to the ciphertext integer *c* using the private key (*n, d*) to produce an integer *em*:

    $$em = \text{RSADP}((n, d), c).^{24}$$

    b. Convert the integer *em* to an encoded message *EM*, a byte string of *nLen* bytes (see Appendix B.1):

    $$EM = \text{I2BS}(em, nLen).$$

4. OAEP decoding:

    a. Apply the selected hash function (see Section 5.1) to compute:

    $$HA = \text{H}(A).$$

    HA is a byte string of *HLen* bytes.

    b. Separate the encoded message *EM* into a single byte *Y*, a byte string *maskedMGFSeed'* of *HLen* bytes, and a byte string *maskedDB'* of $nLen - HLen - 1$ bytes as follows:

    $$EM = Y \,\|\, maskedMGFSeed' \,\|\, maskedDB'.$$

    c. Apply the mask-generation function specified in Section 7.2.2.2 to compute:

    $$mgfSeedMask' = \text{MGF}(maskedDB', HLen).$$

    d. Let $mgfSeed' = maskedMGFSeed' \oplus mgfSeedMask'$.

---

[24] When the private key is represented in the prime-factor or CRT format, appropriate changes are discussed in Section 7.1.2.

e. Apply the mask-generation function specified in Section 7.2.2.2 to compute:

$$dbMask' = \text{MGF}(mgfSeed', nLen - HLen - 1).$$

f. Let $DB' = maskedDB' \oplus dbMask'$.

g. Separate DB' into a byte string HA' of $HLen$ bytes and a byte string X of $nLen - 2HLen - 1$ bytes as follows:

$$DB' = HA' \| X.$$

5. Check for RSA-OAEP decryption errors:

   a. $DecryptErrorFlag = False$.

   b. If Y is not the 00 byte (i.e., the bit string 00000000), then $DecryptErrorFlag = True$.

   c. If HA' does not equal HA, then $DecryptErrorFlag = True$.

   d. If X does not have the form $PS \| 00000001 \| K$, where PS consists of zero or more consecutive 00 bytes, then $DecryptErrorFlag = True$.

   The type(s) of any error(s) found **shall not** be reported. (See the notes below for more information.)

6. Output of the decryption process:

   a. If $DecryptErrorFlag = True$, then output an indication of an (unspecified) decryption error, and exit without further processing. (See the notes below for more information.)

   b. Otherwise, output K, the portion of the byte string X that follows the leading 01 byte.

Output:

K: the recovered keying material (a byte string of at most $nLen - 2HLen - 2$ bytes), or an error indicator.

A routine that implements this operation **shall** destroy any local copies of sensitive input values (including the private key and any sensitive portions of A), any locally stored portions of K, and any other potentially sensitive locally stored values used or produced during the execution of the routine (including $DecryptErrorFlag$, em, EM, HA, Y, $maskedMGFSeed'$, $maskedDB'$, $mgfSeedMask'$, $mfgSeed'$, $dbMask'$, DB', HA', and X). The destruction of these locally stored values **shall** occur prior to or during any exit from the routine – whether exiting because of an error, or exiting normally with the output of K. Note that the requirement for destruction includes any locally stored portions of the recovered keying material.

Notes:

1. Care **should** be taken to ensure that the different error conditions that may be detected in step 5 above cannot be distinguished from one another by an opponent, whether by an error message or by process timing. Otherwise, an opponent may be able to obtain useful

information about the decryption of a chosen ciphertext C, leading to the attack observed by Manger in [Manger 2001]. A single error message **should** be employed and output the same way for each type of decryption error. There **should** be no difference in the observable behavior for the different RSA-OAEP decryption errors.

2. In addition, care **should** be taken to ensure that even if there are no errors, an implementation does not reveal partial information about the encoded message *em* or *EM*. For instance, the observable behavior of the mask-generation function **should not** reveal even partial information about the MGF seed employed in the process (since that could compromise portions of the *maskedDB'* segment of *EM*). An opponent who can reliably obtain particular bits of *EM* for sufficiently many chosen-ciphertext values may be able to obtain the full decryption of an arbitrary ciphertext by applying the bit-security results of Håstad and Näslund [HN 1998].

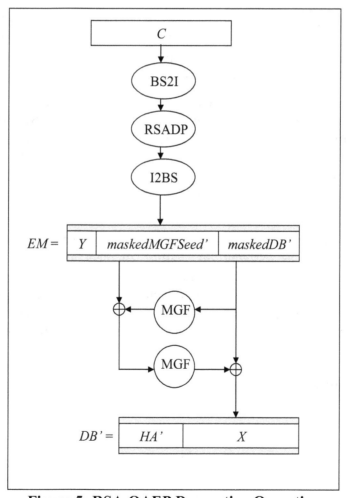

Figure 5: RSA-OAEP Decryption Operation

8 Key-Agreement Schemes

In a key-agreement scheme, two parties, party U and party V, establish keying material over which neither has complete control of the result, but both have influence. This Recommendation provides two families of key-agreement schemes: **KAS1** and **KAS2**. The **KAS1** family consists of the **KAS1-basic** and **KAS1-Party_V-confirmation** schemes, and the **KAS2** family consists of the **KAS2-basic**, **KAS2-Party_V-confirmation**, **KAS2-Party_U-confirmation**, and **KAS2-bilateral-confirmation** schemes. These schemes are based on secret-value encapsulation (see Section 7.2.1).

Key confirmation is included in some of these schemes to provide assurance that the participants share the same keying material; see Section 5.6 for the details of key confirmation. When possible, each party **should** have such assurance. Although other methods are often used to provide this assurance, this Recommendation makes no statement as to the adequacy of these other methods. Key confirmation may also provide assurance of private-key possession.

For each of the **KAS1** and **KAS2** schemes, Party V **shall** have an identifier, ID_V, that has an association with the key pair that is known (or discoverable) and trusted by party U (i.e., there **shall** be a trusted association between ID_V and party V's public key). For the **KAS2** key-agreement schemes, party U **shall** also have such an identifier, ID_U.

A general flow diagram is provided for each key-agreement scheme. The dotted-line arrows represent the distribution of public keys by the parties themselves or by a third party, such as a Certification Authority (CA). The solid-line arrows represent the distribution of nonces or cryptographically protected values that occur during the key-agreement scheme. Note that the flow diagrams in this Recommendation omit explicit mention of various validation checks that are required. The flow diagrams and descriptions in this Recommendation assume a successful completion of the key-agreement process.

For each scheme, there are conditions that must be satisfied to enable proper use of that scheme. These conditions are listed as *assumptions*. Failure to meet all such conditions could yield undesirable results, such as the inability to communicate or the loss of security. As part of the proper implementation of this Recommendation, system users and/or agents trusted to act on their behalf (including application developers, system installers, and system administrators) are responsible for ensuring that all assumptions are satisfied at the time that a key-establishment transaction takes place.

8.1 Common Components for Key Agreement

The key-agreement schemes in this Recommendation have the following common components:

1. RSASVE: RSA secret-value encapsulation, consisting of a generation operation RSASVE.GENERATE and a recovery operation RSASVE.RECOVER (see Section 7.2.1).

2. KDM: A key-derivation method (see Section 5.5).

8.2   KAS1 Key Agreement

For the **KAS1** key-agreement schemes, even if both parties have key-establishment key pairs, only party V's key-establishment key pair is used.

The **KAS1** key-agreement schemes have the following general form:

1. Party U generates a secret value (which will become a shared secret) and a corresponding ciphertext using the RSASVE.GENERATE operation and party V's public key-establishment key, and then sends the ciphertext to party V.

2. Party V recovers the secret value from the ciphertext using the RSASVE.RECOVER operation and its private key-establishment key; the secret value is then considered to be the shared secret. Party V generates a nonce and sends it to party U.

3. Both parties then derive keying material from the shared secret and "other information", including party V's nonce, using a key-derivation method. The length of the keying material that can be agreed on is limited only by the length that can be output by the key-derivation method.

4. If key confirmation (KC) is incorporated into the scheme, then the derived keying material is parsed into two parts, *MacKey* and *KeyData*, and a *MacData* string is formed (see Sections 5.6 and 8.2.3.2.), *MacKey* and *MacData* are used to compute a MAC tag of *MacTagBits* bits (see Sections 5.2.1, 5.2.2, 5.6.1 and 5.6.3), and *MacTag* is sent from party V (the KC provider) to party U (the KC recipient). If the MAC tag computed by party V matches the MAC tag (re)computed by party U, then the successful establishment of keying material is confirmed to party U.

The following schemes are defined:

1. **KAS1-basic,** the basic scheme without key confirmation (see Section 8.2.2).

2. **KAS1-Party_V-confirmation,** a variant of **KAS1-basic** with unilateral key confirmation provided by party V to party U (see Section 8.2.3).

For the security properties of the **KAS1** key-agreement schemes, see Section 10.1.

8.2.1   KAS1 Assumptions

1. Party V has been designated as the owner of a key-establishment key pair that was generated as specified in Section 6.3. Party V has assurance of possession of the correct value for its private key as specified in Section 6.4.1.5.

2. Party U and party V have agreed upon an **approved** key-derivation method (see Section 5.5), as well as an **approved** algorithm to be used with that method (e.g., a specific hash function) and other associated parameters related to the cryptographic elements to be used.

3. If key confirmation is used, party U and party V have agreed upon an **approved** MAC algorithm, auxiliary functions (e.g., a hash algorithm) and associated parameters, including the lengths of *MacKey* and *MacTag* (see Section 5.2).

4. When an identifier is used to label either party during the key-agreement process, both parties are aware of the particular identifier employed for that purpose. In particular, when

an identifier is used to label party V during the key-agreement process, that identifier's association with party V's public key is trusted by party U. When an identifier is used to label party U during the key-agreement process, it has been selected/assigned in accordance with the requirements of the protocol relying upon the use of the key-agreement scheme.

5. Party U has obtained assurance of the validity of party V's public key, as specified in Section 6.4.2.

The following is an assumption for using any keying material derived during a **KAS1** key-agreement scheme for purposes beyond those of the scheme itself.

Party U has obtained (or will obtain) assurance that party V is (or was) in possession of the private key corresponding to the public key used during the key-agreement transaction, as specified in Section 6.4.2.3.

This assumption recognizes the possibility that assurance of private-key possession may be provided/obtained by means of key confirmation performed as part of a particular **KAS1** transaction.

8.2.2 KAS1-basic

KAS1-basic is the basic key-agreement scheme in the **KAS1** family. In this scheme, party V does not contribute to the formation of the shared secret; instead, a nonce is used as a party V-selected contribution to the key-derivation method, ensuring that both parties influence the derived keying material.

Let ($PubKey_V$, $PrivKey_V$) be party V's key-establishment key pair. Let $KBits$ be the intended length in bits of the keying material to be established. The parties **shall** perform the following or an equivalent sequence of steps, as illustrated in Figure 6.

Party U		Party V
		($PubKey_V$, $PrivKey_V$)
Obtain party V's public key-establishment key	$PubKey_V$ ← − − − −	
(Z, C) = RSASVE.GENERATE($PubKey_V$)	C →	Z = RSASVE.RECOVER($PrivKey_V$, C)
Compute DerivedKeyingMaterial and Destroy Z	N_V ←	Compute DerivedKeyingMaterial and Destroy Z

Figure 6: KAS1-basic Scheme

Party U **shall** execute the following key-agreement steps in order to a) establish a shared secret Z with party V, and b) derive secret keying material from Z.

Actions: Party U generates a shared secret and derives secret keying material as follows:

1. Use the RSASVE.GENERATE operation in Section 7.2.1.2 to generate a secret value Z and a corresponding ciphertext C using party V's public key-establishment key, $PubKey_V$. Note that the secret value Z will become a shared secret when recovered by Party V.

2. Send the ciphertext C to party V.

3. Obtain party V's nonce N_V from party V. If N_V is not available, return an error indicator without performing the remaining actions.

4. Assemble the *OtherInput* for key derivation, including the required nonce, N_V, and any other requisite information (see Section 5.5).

5. Use the agreed-upon key-derivation method (see Section 5.5) to derive secret keying material of the agreed-upon length from the shared secret value Z and *OtherInput* (see step 4). If the key-derivation method outputs an error indicator, return an error indicator without performing the remaining actions.

6. Output the *DerivedKeyingMaterial*.

Any local copies of Z, *OtherInput*, *DerivedKeyingMaterial* and any intermediate values used during the execution of party U's actions **shall** be destroyed prior to the early termination of the actions due to an error, or (in the absence of errors), prior to or during the the completion of step 6.

Party V **shall** execute the following key-agreement steps in order to a) establish a shared secret Z with party U, and b) derive secret keying material from Z.

Actions: Party V obtains the shared secret and derives secret keying material as follows:

1. Receive a ciphertext C from party U.

2. Use the RSASVE.RECOVER operation in Section 7.2.1.3 to recover the secret value Z from the ciphertext C using the private key-establishment key, *PrivKey$_V$*; hereafter, Z is considered to be a shared secret. If the call to RSASVE.RECOVER outputs an error indicator, return an error indicator without performing the remaining actions.

3. Obtain a nonce N_V (see Section 5.4), and send N_V to party U.

4. Assemble the *OtherInpu,* for key derivation using the nonce N_V and the identifiers ID_U and ID_V, if available (see Section 5.5).

5. Use the agreed-upon key-derivation method to derive secret keying material with the agreed upon length from the shared secret value Z and other input. If the key-derivation method outputs an error indicator, return an error indicator without performing the remaining actions.

6. Output the *DerivedKeyingMaterial*.

Any local copies of Z, *PrivKey$_V$*, *OtherInput DerivedKeyingMaterial* and any intermediate values used during the execution of party V's actions **shall** be destroyed prior to the early termination of the actions due to an error, or (in the absence of errors) prior to or during the the completion of step 6.

The messages may be sent in a different order, i.e., N_V may be sent before C.

It is extremely important that an implementation not reveal any sensitive information. It is also important to conceal partial information about the shared secret Z to prevent chosen-ciphertext attacks on the secret-value encapsulation scheme.

8.2.3 KAS1 Key Confirmation

The **KAS1-Party_V-confirmation** scheme is based on the **KAS1-basic** scheme.

8.2.3.1 KAS1 Key-Confirmation Components

The components for **KAS1** key agreement with key confirmation are the components listed in Section 8.1, plus the following:

MAC: A message authentication code algorithm with the following parameters (see Section 5.2),

a. *MacKeyLen*: the byte length of *MacKey*, and

b. *MacTagLen*: the byte length of *MacTag*. (*MacTagBits*, as used in Section 5.2, is equal to $8 \times MacTagLen$.)

MacKey **shall** be the first *MacKeyLen* bytes of the keying material and **shall** be used only for the key-confirmation operation of a single transaction. For **KAS1** key confirmation, the length of the derived keying material **shall** be at least *MacKeyLen* bytes in length. The keying material is usually longer than *MacKeyLen* bytes so that other keying material is available for subsequent operations.

8.2.3.2 KAS1-Party_V-confirmation

Figure 7 depicts a typical flow for a **KAS1** scheme with unilateral key confirmation from party V to party U. In this scheme, party V and party U assume the roles of key-confirmation provider and recipient, respectively. The successful completion of the key-confirmation process provides party U with a) assurance that party V has derived the same secret Z value, and b) assurance that party V has actively participated in the process.

Party U		Party V
		$(PubKey_V, PrivKey_V)$
Obtain party V's public key-establishment key	$PubKey_V$ ◄ ─ ─ ─ ─ ─	
$(Z, C) = $ RSASVE.GENERATE$(PubKey_V)$	C ───────►	$Z = $ RSASVE.RECOVER$(PrivKey_V, C)$
Compute *DerivedKeyingMaterial* and Destroy Z	N_V ◄───────	Compute *DerivedKeyingMaterial* and Destroy Z
$MacTag_V = ?$ $T_{MacTagBits}[\mathrm{MAC}(MacKey, MacData_V)]$	◄─────── $MacTag_V$	$MacTag_V = $ $T_{MacTagBits}[\mathrm{MAC}(MacKey, MacData_V)]$

Figure 7: KAS1-Party-V-confirmation Scheme (From Party V to Party U)

Each party first performs the appropriate steps of the **KAS1-basic** scheme as described in Section 8.2.2.

To provide (and receive) key confirmation (as described in Section 5.6.1), both parties set $EphemData_V = N_V$, and $EphemData_U = C$:

Party V provides $MacTag_V$ to party U (as specified in Section 5.6.1, with $P = V$ and $R = U$), where $MacTag_V$ is computed (as specified in Section 5.2.1) using

$$MacData_V = \text{``KC\_1\_V''} \parallel ID_V \parallel ID_U \parallel N_V \parallel C\{ \parallel Text_V\}.$$

Party U uses the identical format and values to compute $T_{MacTagBits}[MAC(MacKey, MacData_V)$, and then verify that it matches the $MacTag_V$ value provided by party V.

The *MacKey* used during key confirmation **shall** be destroyed by party V immediately after the computation of $MacTag_V$, and by party U immediately after the verification of the received $MacTag_V$ or a (final) determination that the received $MacTag_V$ is in error.

Certain messages may be combined or sent in a different order (e.g., N_V and $MacTag_V$ may be sent together, or N_V may be sent before C).

8.3   KAS2 Key Agreement

In this family of key-agreement schemes, key-establishment key pairs are used by both party U and party V.

The schemes in this family have the following general form:

1. Party U generates a secret value (which will become a component of the shared secret) and a corresponding ciphertext using the RSASVE.GENERATE operation and party V's public key-establishment key, and sends the ciphertext to party V.

2. Party V recovers party U's secret component from the ciphertext received from party U using the RSASVE.RECOVER operation and its private key-establishment key.

3. Party V generates a secret value (which will become a second component of the shared secret) and the corresponding ciphertext using the RSASVE.GENERATE operation and party U's public key-establishment key, and sends the ciphertext to party U.

4. Party U recovers party V's secret component from the ciphertext received from party V using the RSASVE.RECOVER operation and its private key-establishment key.

5. Both parties concatenate the two secret components to form the shared secret, and then derive keying material from the shared secret and "other information" using a key-derivation method. The length of the keying material that can be agreed on is limited only by the length that can be output by the key-derivation method.

6. Party U and/or party V may additionally provide key confirmation. If key confirmation is incorporated, then the derived keying material is parsed into two parts, *MacKey* and *KeyData*. *MacKey* is then used to compute a MAC tag of *MacTagLen* bytes on *MacData* (see Sections 5.2.1, 5.2.2, 5.6.1 and 5.6.3). Key confirmation may be either unilateral or bilateral. When key confirmation is performed, a *MacTag* is sent from a KC provider to a KC recipient.

   When unilateral key confirmation in performed: One party assumes the role of the KC provider, and the other party assumes the role of the KC recipient. If the MAC tag computed by the provider matches the MAC tag computed by the recipient, then the successful establishment of keying material is confirmed by the recipient.

When bilateral key confirmation is performed: The key confirmation process requires two interactions (e.g., two messages). In the first interaction, one party assumes the role of the KC provider, and the other party assumes the role of the KC recipient. In the second interaction, the roles are reversed. If each party acting as a recipient determines that the computed MAC tag matches the MAC tag provided by the other party (acting as the provider), then the successful establishment of keying material is confirmed by both parties, and each party has obtained assurance that the other party has actively participated in the transaction.

The following schemes are defined:

1. **KAS2-basic,** the basic scheme without key confirmation (see Section 8.3.2).

2. **KAS2-Party_V-confirmation,** a variant of **KAS2-basic** with unilateral key confirmation provided by party V to party U (see Section 8.3.3.2).

3. **KAS2-Party_U-confirmation,** a variant of **KAS2-basic** with unilateral key confirmation probided by party U to party V (see Section 8.3.3.3).

4. **KAS2-bilateral-confirmation,** a variant of **KAS2-basic** with bilateral key confirmation between party U and party V (see Section 8.3.3.4).

For the security properties of the **KAS2** key-agreement schemes, see Section 10.2.

8.3.1 KAS2 Assumptions

1. Each party has been designated as the owner of a key-establishment key pair that was generated as specified in Section 6.3. Prior to or during the key-agreement process, each party has obtained assurance of its possession of the correct value for its own private key as specified in Section 6.4.1.5.

2. The parties have agreed upon an **approved** key-derivation method (see Section 5.5), as well as an **approved** algorithm to be used with that method (e.g., a specific hash function) and other associated parameters to be used for key derivation.

3. If key confirmation is used, party U and party V have agreed upon an **approved** MAC algorithm and associated parameters, including the lengths of *MacKey* and *MacTag* (see Section 5.2). The parties must also agree on whether one party or both parties will send *MacTag*, and in what order.

4. When an identifier is used to label a party during the key-agreement process, that identifier has a trusted association to that party's public key. (In other words, whenever both the identifier and public key of one participant are employed in the key-agreement process, they are associated in a manner that is trusted by the other participant.) When an identifier is used to label a party during the key-agreement process, both parties are aware of the particular identifier employed for that purpose.

5. Each party has obtained assurance of the validity of the public keys that are used during the transaction, as specified in Section 6.4.2.3.

The following is an assumption for using any keying material derived during a **KAS2** key-agreement scheme for purposes beyond those of the scheme itself.

Each party has obtained (or will obtain) assurance that the other party is (or was) in possession of the private key corresponding to their public key that was used during the key-agreement transaction, as specified in Section 6.4.2.3.

This assumption recognizes the possibility that assurance of private-key possession may be provided/obtained by means of key confirmation performed as part of a particular **KAS2** transaction.

8.3.2 KAS2-basic

Figure 8 depicts the typical flow for the **KAS2-basic** scheme. The parties exchange secret values that are concatenated to form the mutually determined shared secret to be input to the key-derivation method.

Party U **shall** execute the following key-agreement steps in order to a) establish a mutually determined shared secret Z with party V, and b) derive secret keying material from Z.

Party U		Party V
$(PubKey_U, PrivKey_U)$		$(PubKey_V, PrivKey_V)$
Obtain party V's public key-establishment key	$PubKey_V$ ← — — —	
	$PubKey_U$ — — — →	Obtain party U's public key-establishment key
$(Z_U, C_U) =$ RSASVE.GENERATE($PubKey_V$)	C_U ⟶	$Z_U =$ RSASVE.RECOVER($PrivKey_V, C_U$)
$Z_V =$ RSASVE.RECOVER($PrivKey_U, C_V$)	C_V ←	$(Z_V, C_V) =$ RSASVE.GENERATE($PubKey_U$)
$Z = Z_U \parallel Z_V$		$Z = Z_U \parallel Z_V$
Compute *DerivedKeyingMaterial* and destroy Z		Compute *DerivedKeyingMaterial* and destroy Z

Figure 8: KAS2-basic Scheme

Actions: Party U generates a shared secret and derives secret keying material as follows:

1. Use the RSASVE.GENERATE operation in Section 7.2.1.2 to generate a secret value Z_U and a corresponding ciphertext C_U using party V's public key-establishment key $PubKey_V$.

2. Send the ciphertext C_U to party V.

3. Receive a ciphertext C_V from party V. If C_V is not available, return an error indicator without performing the remaining actions.

4. Use the RSASVE.RECOVER operation in Section 7.2.1.3 to recover Z_V from the ciphertext C_V using the private key-establishment key $PrivKey_U$. If the call to RSASVE.RECOVER

outputs an error indicator, return an error indicator without performing the remaining actions.

5. Construct the mutually determined shared secret Z from Z_U and Z_V

$$Z = Z_U \parallel Z_V.$$

6. Assemble the *OtherInput* for key derivation, including all requisite information (see Section 5.5).

7 Use the agreed-upon key-derivation method (see Section 5.5) to derive secret keying material with the specified length from the shared secret Z and other input. If the key-derivation method outputs an error indicator, return an error indicator without performing the remaining actions.

8. Output the *DerivedKeyingMaterial*.

Any local copies of Z, Z_U, Z_V, *PrivKey$_U$*, *OtherInput*, *DerivedKeyingMaterial* and any intermediate values used during the execution of party U's actions **shall** be destroyed prior to the early termination of the actions due to an error, or (in the absence of errors), prior to or during the completion of step 8.

Party V **shall** execute the following key-agreement steps in order to a) establish a mutually determined shared secret Z with party U, and b) derive secret keying material from Z.

Actions: Party V generates a shared secret and derives secret keying material as follows:

1. Receive a ciphertext C_U from party U.

2. Use the RSASVE.RECOVER operation in Section 7.2.1.3 to recover Z_U from the ciphertext C_U using the private key-establishment key *PrivKey$_U$*. If the call to RSASVE.RECOVER outputs an error indicator, return an error indicator without performing the remaining actions.

3. Use the RSASVE.GENERATE operation in Section 7.2.1.2 to generate a secret value Z_V and a corresponding ciphertext C_V using party U's public key-establishment key *PubKey$_U$*.

4. Send the ciphertext C_V to party U.

5. Construct the mutually determined shared secret Z from Z_U and Z_V

$$Z = Z_U \parallel Z_V.$$

6. Assemble the *OtherInput* for key derivation, including all requisite information (see Section 5.5).

7. Use the agreed-upon key-derivation method (see Section 5.5) to derive *KBits* of secret keying material *DerivedKeyingMaterial* from the shared secret Z and *OtherInput*. If the key-derivation method outputs an error indicator, return an error indicator without performing the remaining actions.

8. Output the *DerivedKeyingMaterial*.

Any local copies of Z, Z_U, Z_V, *PrivKey$_V$*, *OtherInput*, *DerivedKeyingMaterial* and any intermediate values used during the execution of party V's actions **shall** be destroyed prior to the early termination of the actions due to an error, or (in the absence of errors), prior to or during the completion of step 8.

The messages may be sent in a different order, i.e., C_V may be sent before C_U.

It is extremely important that an implementation not reveal any sensitive information. It is also important to conceal partial information about Z_U, Z_V and Z to prevent chosen-ciphertext attacks on the secret-value encapsulation scheme. In particular, the observable behavior of the key-agreement process **should not** reveal partial information about the shared secret Z.

8.3.3 KAS2 Key Confirmation

The **KAS2** key-confirmation schemes are based on the **KAS2-basic** scheme.

8.3.3.1 KAS2 Key-Confirmation Components

The components for **KAS2** key agreement with key confirmation are the components in Section 8.1, plus the following:

MAC: A message authentication code algorithm with the following parameters (see Section 5.2)

     a. *MacKeyLen*: the byte length of *MacKey*.

     b. *MacTagLen*: the byte length of *MacTag*. (*MacTagBits*, as used in Section 5.2, is equal to 8 × *MacTagLen*.)

MacKey **shall** be the first *MacKeyLen* bytes of the keying material and **shall** be used only for the key-confirmation operation of a single transaction. For **KAS2** key confirmation, the length of the keying material **shall** be at least *MacKeyLen* bytes. The keying material is usually longer than *MacKeyLen* bytes so that other keying material is available for subsequent operations.

8.3.3.2 KAS2-Party_V-confirmation

Figure 9 depicts a typical flow for a **KAS2** scheme with unilateral key confirmation from party V to party U. In this scheme, party V and party U assume the roles of the key-confirmation provider and recipient, respectively. The successful completion of the key-confirmation process provides party U with a) assurance that party V has derived the same secret Z value, and b) assurance that party V has actively participated in the process.

Party U		Party V
$(PubKey_U, PrivKey_U)$		$(PubKey_V, PrivKey_V)$
Obtain party V's public key-establishment key	$PubKey_V$ ← — — —	
	$PubKey_U$ — — — →	Obtain party U's public key establishment-key
$(Z_U, C_U) =$ RSASVE.Generate($PubKey_V$)	C_U ⟶	Z_U = RSASVE.Recover($PrivKey_V$, C_U)
$Z_V =$ RSASVE.RECOVER($PrivKey_U$, C_V)	C_V ←	$(Z_V, C_V) =$ RSASVE.GENERATE($PubKey_U$)
$Z = Z_U \| Z_V$		$Z = Z_U \| Z_V$
Compute *DerivedKeyingMaterial* = *MacKey* || *KeyData* and destroy Z		Compute *DerivedKeyingMaterial* = *MacKey* || *KeyData* and destroy Z
$MacTag_V$ =? $T_{MacTagBits}$[MAC(*MacKey*, *MacData$_V$*)]	$MacTag_V$ ←	$MacTag_V =$ $T_{MacTagBits}$[MAC(*MacKey*, *MacData$_V$*)]

Figure 9: KAS2-Party_V-confirmation Scheme (from Party V to Party U)

Each party first performs the appropriate steps of the **KAS2-basic** scheme as described in Section 8.3.2.

To provide (and receive) key confirmation (as described in Section 5.6.1), both parties set *EphemData$_V$* = C_V, and *EphemData$_U$* = C_U.

Party V provides *MacTag$_V$* to party U (as specified in Section 5.6.1, with P = V and R = U), where *MacTag$_V$* is computed (as specified in Section 5.2.1) on

$$MacData_V = \text{"KC\_1\_V"} \| ID_V \| ID_U \| C_V \| C_U \{ \| Text_V \}.$$

Party U (the KC recipient) uses the identical format and values to compute $T_{MacTagBits}$[MAC(*MacKey*, *MacData$_V$*)] and then verify that it equals *MacTag$_V$* as provided by party V.

The MAC key used during key confirmation (i.e., *MacKey*) **shall** be destroyed by party V immediately after the computation of *MacTag$_V$*, and by party U immediately after the verification of the received *MacTag$_V$* or a (final) determination that the received *MacTag$_V$* is in error.

Certain messages may be combined or sent in a different order (e.g., C_V and *MacTag$_V$* may be sent together, or C_V may be sent before C_U).

8.3.3.3 KAS2-Party_U-confirmation

Figure 10 depicts a typical flow for a **KAS2** scheme with unilateral key confirmation from party U to party V. In this scheme, party U and party V assume the roles of key-confirmation provider and recipient, respectively. The successful completion of the key-confirmation process provides party V with a) assurance that party U has derived the same secret Z value, and b) assurance that party U has actively participated in the process.

Party U		Party V
$(PubKey_U, PrivKey_U)$		$(PubKey_V, PrivKey_V)$
Obtain party V's public key-establishment key	$PubKey_V$ $\leftarrow - - -$	
	$PubKey_U$ $- - - \rightarrow$	Obtain party U's public key-establishment key
$(Z_U, C_U) =$ RSASVE.GENERATE($PubKey_V$)	C_U $\longrightarrow$	$Z_U =$ RSASVE.RECOVER($PrivKey_V$, C_U)
$Z_V =$ RSASVE.RECOVER($PrivKey_U$, C_V)	C_V $\longleftarrow$	$(Z_V, C_V) =$ RSASVE.GENERATE($PubKey_U$)
$Z = Z_U \| Z_V$		$Z = Z_U \| Z_V$
Compute $DerivedKeyingMaterial =$ $MacKey \| KeyData$ and destroy Z		Compute $DerivedKeyingMaterial =$ $MacKey \| KeyData$ and destroy Z
$MacTag_U =$ $T_{MacTagBits}[\text{MAC}(MacKey, MacData_U)]$	$MacTag_U$ $\longrightarrow$	$MacTag_U =?$ $T_{MacTagBits}[\text{MAC}(MacKey, MacData_U)]$

Figure 10: KAS2-Party_U-confirmation Scheme (from Party U to Party V)

Each party first performs the appropriate steps of the **KAS2-basic** scheme as described in Section 8.3.2.

To provide (and receive) key confirmation (as described in Section 5.6.1), both parties set $EphemData_V = C_V$, and $EphemData_U = C_U$.

Party U provides $MacTag_U$ to party V (as specified in Section 5.6.1, with $P = $ U and $R = $ V), where $MacTag_U$ is computed (as specified in Section 5.2.1) on

$$MacData_U = \text{``KC\_1\_U''} \| ID_U \| ID_V \| C_U \| C_V\{ \| Text_U\}.$$

Party V (the KC recipient) uses the identical format and values to compute $T_{MacTagBits}[\text{MAC}(MacKey, MacData_U)]$ and then verify that it matches the $MacTag_U$ value provided by party U.

The MAC key used during key confirmation **shall** be destroyed by party U immediately after the computation of $MacTag_U$, and by party V immediately after the verification of the received $MacTag_U$ or a (final) determination that the received $MacTag_U$ is in error.

Note that C_V may be sent before C_U, in which case C_U and $MacTag_U$ may be sent together.

8.3.3.4 KAS2-bilateral-confirmation

Figure 11 depicts a typical flow for a KAS2 scheme with bilateral key confirmation. In this scheme, party U and party V assume the roles of both the KC provider and recipient in order to obtain bilateral key confirmation. The successful completion of the key-confirmation process provides each party with a) assurance that other party has derived the same secret Z value, and b) assurance that the other party has actively participated in the process.

Party U		Party V
$(PubKey_U, PrivKey_U)$		$(PubKey_V, PrivKey_V)$
Obtain party V's public key-establishment key	$PubKey_V$ $\leftarrow - - -$	
	$PubKey_U$ $- - - \rightarrow$	Obtain party U's public key-establishment key
$(Z_U, C_U) =$ RSASVE.GENERATE$(PubKey_V)$	C_U $\longrightarrow$	$Z_U =$ RSASVE.RECOVER$(PrivKey_V, C_U)$
$Z_V =$ RSASVE.RECOVER$(PrivKey_U, C_V)$	C_V $\longleftarrow$	$(Z_V, C_V) =$ RSASVE.GENERATE$(PubKey_U)$
$Z = Z_U \| Z_V$		$Z = Z_U \| Z_V$
Compute *DerivedKeyingMaterial* = *MacKey* | *KeyData* and destroy Z		Compute *DerivedKeyingMaterial* = *MacKey* | *KeyData* and destroy Z
$MacTag_V =?$ $T_{MacTagBits}[\text{MAC}(MacKey, MacData_V)]$	$MacTag_V$ $\longleftarrow$	$MacTag_V =$ $T_{MacTagBits}[\text{MAC}(MacKey, MacData_V)]$
$MacTag_U =$ $T_{MacTagBits}[\text{MAC}(MacKey, MacData_U)]$	$MacTag_U$ $\longrightarrow$	$MacTag_U =?$ $T_{MacTagBits}[\text{MAC}(MacKey, MacData_U)]$

Figure 11: KAS2-bilateral-confirmation Scheme

Each party first performs the appropriate steps of the **KAS2-basic** scheme as described in Section 8.3.2.

To provide bilateral key confirmation (as described in Section 5.6.2), party U and party V exchange and verify *MacTags* that have been computed (as specified in Section 5.6.1) using $EphemData_U = C_U$, and $EphemData_V = C_V$.

Party V provides $MacTag_V$ to party U (as specified in Section 5.6.1, with P = V and R = U); $MacTag_V$ is computed by party V (and verified by party U) using

$$MacData_V = \text{``KC\_2\_V''} \| ID_V \| ID_U \| C_V \| C_U \{ \| Text_V \}.$$

Party U provides $MacTag_U$ to party V (as specified in Section 5.6.1, with P = U and R = V); $MacTag_U$ is computed by party U (and verified by party V) using

$$MacData_U = \text{``KC\_2\_U''} \parallel ID_U \parallel ID_V \parallel C_U \parallel C_V \{ \parallel Text_U \}.$$

The MAC key used during key confirmation **shall** be destroyed by each party immediately following its use to compute and verify the MAC tags used for key confirmation. Once party U has computed $MacTag_U$ and has either verified the received $MacTag_V$ or made a (final) determination that the received $MacTag_U$ is in error, party U **shall** immediately destroy its copy of $MacKey$. Similarly, after party V has computed $MacTag_V$ and has either verified the received $MacTag_U$ or made a (final) determination that the received $MacTag_U$ is in error, party V **shall** immediately destroy its copy of $MacKey$.

Certain messages may be sent in a different order (and/or combined with others), e.g., C_V may be sent before C_U and/or $MacTag_V$ may be sent before $MacTag_U$.

9   Key-Transport Schemes

In a key-transport scheme, two parties, the *sender* and *receiver*, establish keying material selected by the sender. The keying material may be cryptographically bound to additional input (see Section 9.1).

In this Recommendation, the **KTS-OAEP** family of key-transport schemes is specified (see Section 9.2). In addition, a hybrid method for key transport is discussed whereby a key-establishment scheme specified in this Recommendation is followed by a key-wrapping scheme (see Section 9.3).

Key confirmation is included in one of the **KTS-OAEP** schemes to provide assurance to the sender that the participants share the same keying material (see Section 5.6 for further details on key confirmation).

A general flow diagram is provided for each **KTS-OAEP** key-transport scheme. The dotted-line arrows represent the distribution of public keys by the parties themselves or by a third party, such as a Certification Authority (CA). The solid-line arrows represent the distribution of cryptographically protected values that occur during the key-transport or key-confirmation process. Note that the flow diagrams in this Recommendation omit explicit mention of various validation checks that are required. The flow diagrams and descriptions in this Recommendation assume a successful completion of the key-transport process.

As in Section 8, there are conditions that must be satisfied for each key-transport scheme to enable the proper use of that scheme. These conditions are listed as *assumptions*. Failure to meet any of these conditions could yield undesirable results, such as the inability to communicate or the loss of security. As part of the proper implementation of this Recommendation, system users and/or agents trusted to act on their behalf (including application developers, system installers, and system administrators) are responsible for ensuring that all assumptions are satisfied at the time that a key-establishment transaction takes place.

9.1   Additional Input

Additional input to the key-transport process may be employed to ensure that the keying material is adequately "bound" to the context of the key-transport transaction. The use of additional input, A, is explicitly supported by the key-transport schemes specified in Section 9.2. Each party to a key-transport transaction **shall** know whether or not additional input is employed in that transaction.

Context-specific information that may be appropriate for inclusion in the additional input is listed in Section 5.5.2. (The suggestions for the content of *FixedInfo* apply to the additional input as well.)

Both parties to the key-transport transaction **shall** know the format of the additional input, A, and **shall** acquire A in time to use it as required by the scheme. The methods used for formatting and distributing the additional input are application-defined. System users and/or agents trusted to act on their behalf **should** determine that the information selected for inclusion in A and the methods used for formatting and distributing A meet the security requirements of those users.

9.2   KTS-OAEP: Key-Transport Using RSA-OAEP

The KTS-OAEP family of key-transport schemes is based on the RSA-OAEP encrypt and decrypt operations (see Section 7.2.2), which are, in turn, based on the asymmetric encryption and decryption primitives, RSAEP and RSADP (see Section 7.1). In this family, only party V's key pair is used.

The key-transport schemes of this family have the following general form:

1. Party U (the sender) encrypts the keying material (and possibly additional input – see Section 7.2.2.3) to be transported using the RSA-OAEP.ENCRYPT operation and party V's (the receiver's) public key-establishment key to produce ciphertext, and sends the ciphertext to party V.

2. Party V decrypts the ciphertext using its private key-establishment key and the RSA-OAEP.DECRYPT operation to recover the transported keying material (see Section 7.2.2.4).

3. If key confirmation is incorporated, then the transported keying material is parsed into two parts, a transaction-specific (random) value for *MacKey*, followed by *KeyData* (see Section 5.6.1). The *Mackey* portion of the keying material and an **approved** MAC algorithm are used by each party to compute a MAC tag (of an appropriate, agreed-upon length) on what should be the same *MacData* (see Sections 5.6 and 9.2.4.2). The MAC tag computed by party V (the key-confirmation provider) is sent to party U (the key-confirmation recipient). If the value of the MAC tag sent by party V matches the MAC tag value computed by party U, then party U obtains a confirmation of the success of the key-transport transaction.

The common components of the schemes in the KTS-OAEP family are listed in Section 9.2.2. The following schemes are then defined:

1. **KTS-OAEP-basic**, the basic scheme without key confirmation (see Section 9.2.3).

2. **KTS-OAEP-Party_V-confirmation**, a variant of **KTS-OAEP-basic** with unilateral key confirmation from party V to party U (see Section 9.2.4).

For the security attributes of the KTS-OAEP family, see Section 10.3.

9.2.1   KTS-OAEP Assumptions

1. Party V has been designated as the owner of a key-establishment key pair that was generated as specified in Section 6.3. Party V has obtained assurance of its possession of the correct value for its private key as specified in Section 6.4.1.5.

2. The parties have agreed upon an **approved** hash function, *hash*, appropriate for use with the mask-generation function used by RSA-OAEP, as well as an **approved** hash function, H, used to hash the additional input (see Sections 5.1, and 7.2.2). The same hash function may be used for both functions.

3. Prior to or during the transport process, the sender and receiver have either agreed upon the form and content of the additional input *A* (a byte string to be cryptographically bound to the transported keying material so that the ciphertext is a function of both values), or agreed that *A* will be a null string (see Section 9.1).

4. If key confirmation is used, the parties have agreed upon an **approved** MAC algorithm and associated parameters, including the lengths of *MacKey* and *MacTag* (see Section 5.2).

5. When an identifier is used to label either party during the key-transport process, both parties are aware of the particular identifier employed for that purpose. In particular, the association of the identifier used to label party V with party V's public key is trusted by party U. When an identifier is used to label party U during the key-transport process, it has been selected/assigned in accordance with the requirements of the protocol relying upon the use of the key-transport scheme.

6. Party U has obtained assurance of the validity of party V's public key, as specified in Section 6.4.2.

7. Prior to or during the key-transport process, party U has obtained (or will obtain) assurance that party V is (or was) in possession of the (correct) private key corresponding to the public key-establishment key used during the transaction, as specified in Section 6.4.2.

8. Prior to or during the key-transport process, the keying material to be transported has been/is determined and has a format as specified in Section 9.

9.2.2 Common components

The schemes in the **KTS-OAEP** family have the following common component:

1. RSA-OAEP: asymmetric operations, consisting of an encryption operation RSA-OAEP.ENCRYPT and a decryption operation RSA-OAEP.DECRYPT (see Section 7.2.2).

9.2.3 KTS-OAEP-basic

KTS-OAEP-basic is the basic key-transport scheme in the KTS-OAEP family without key confirmation.

Let (*PubKey$_V$*, *PrivKey$_V$*) be party V's (the receiver's) key-establishment key pair. Let K be the keying material to be transported from party U (the sender) to party V; note that the length of K is restricted by the length of the RSA modulus and the length of the output of the hash-function used to hash the additional input during the RSA-OAEP process (see Section 7.2.2.3). The parties **shall** perform the following or an equivalent sequence of steps, which are also illustrated in Figure 12.

Party U		Party V
K to be transported		(*PubKey$_V$*, *PrivKey$_V$*)
Obtain party V's public key-establishment key	*PubKey$_V$* ← — — —	
$C =$ RSA-OAEP. ENCRYPT(*PubKey$_V$*, K, A)	C ⟶	$K =$ RSA-OAEP. DECRYPT(*PrivKey$_V$*, C, A)

Figure 12: KTS-OAEP-basic Scheme

Party U **shall** execute the following steps in order to transport keying material to party V.

90

Party U Actions:

1. Encrypt the keying material K using party V's public key-establishment key $PubKey_V$ and the additional input A, to produce a ciphertext C (see Section 7.2.2.3):

$$C = \text{RSA-OAEP.ENCRYPT}(PubKey_V, K, A).$$

2. If an error indication has been returned, then return an error indication without performing the remaining actions.

3. Send the ciphertext C to party V.

Any local copies of K, A, and any intermediate values used during the execution of party U's actions **shall** be destroyed prior to the early termination of the actions due to an error, or (in the absence of errors), prior to or during the the completion of step 3.

Party V **shall** execute the following steps when receiving keys transported from party U.

Party V Actions:

1. Receive the ciphertext C.

2. Decrypt the ciphertext C using the private key-establishment key $PrivKey_V$ and the additional input A, to recover the transported keying material K (see Section 7.2.2.4):

$$K = \text{RSA-OAEP.DECRYPT}(PrivKey_V, C, A).$$

   If the decryption operation outputs an error indicator, return an error indication without performing the remaining action.

3. Output K.

Any local copies of K, $PrivKey_V$, A, and any intermediate values used during the execution of party V's actions **shall** be destroyed prior to the early termination of the actions due to an error, or (in the absence of errors), prior to or during the the completion of step 3.

9.2.4 KTS-OAEP Key Confirmation

The **KES-OAEP-Party_V-confirmation** scheme is based on the **KTS-OAEP-basic scheme**.

9.2.4.1 KTS-OAEP Common Components for Key Confirmation

The components for **KTS-OAEP** with key confirmation are the same as for **KTS-OAEP-basic** (see Section 9.2.2), plus the following:

MAC: A message authentication code algorithm with the following parameters (see Section 5.2):

    a. *MacKeyLen*: the byte length of *MacKey*.

    b. *MacTagLen*: the byte length of *MacTag*. (*MacTagBits*, as used in Section 5.2, is equal to 8 × *MacTagLen*.)

MacKey **shall** be the first *MacKeyLen* bytes of the keying material and **shall** be used only for the key-confirmation operation. For **KTS-OAEP** key confirmation, the length of the keying material **shall** be at least *MacKeyLen* bytes, and usually longer so that keying material other than *MacKey* is available for subsequent operations.

9.2.4.2 KTS-OAEP-Party_V-confirmation

KTS-OAEP-Party_V-confirmation is a variant of **KTS-OAEP-basic** with unilateral key confirmation from party V to party U. The successful completion of the key-confirmation process provides party U with a) assurance that party V has derived the same secret Z value, and b) assurance that party V has actively participated in the process.

Figure 13 depicts a typical flow for the **KTS-OAEP-Party_V-confirmation** scheme. In this scheme, party V and party U assume the roles of key-confirmation provider and recipient, respectively.

Party U		Party V
$K = MacKey \parallel KeyData$		$(PubKey_V, PrivKey_V)$
Obtain party V's public key-establishment key	$PubKey_V$ ← — — —	
$C =$ RSA-OAEP.Encrypt($PubKey_V$, K, A)	C ⟶	$K =$ RSA-OAEP.Decrypt($PrivKey_V$, C, A)
		$MacKey \parallel KeyData = K$
$MacTag_V$ **Error! Bookmark not defined.**=? $T_{MacTagBits}$[MAC(*MacKey*, $MacData_V$)]	$MacTag_V$ ←	$MacTag_V$ **Error! Bookmark not defined.**= $T_{MacTagBits}$[MAC(*MacKey*, $MacData_V$)]

Figure 13: KTS-OAEP-Party_V-confirmation Scheme

Each party first performs the appropriate steps of the **KTS-OAEP-basic** scheme as described in Section 9.2.3.

To provide (and receive) key confirmation (as described in Section 5.6.1), both parties form

$$MacData \text{ with } EphemData_V = Null, \text{ and } EphemData_U = C.$$

Party V provides $MacTag_V$ to party U (as specified in Section 5.6.1, with $P = V$ and $R = U$), where $MacTag_V$ is computed (as specified in Section 5.2.1) using

$$MacData_V = \text{``KC\_1\_V''} \parallel ID_V \parallel ID_U \parallel Null \parallel C\{ \parallel Text_V\}.$$

Party U uses the identical format and values to compute $T_{MacTagBits}[\text{MAC}(MacKey, MacData_V)]$ and then verify that it matches the $MacTag_V$ value provided by party V.

The MAC tag used during key confirmation **shall** be destroyed by party V immediately after the computation of $MacTag_V$, and by party U immediately after the verification of the received $MacTag_V$ or a (final) determination that the received $MacTag_V$ is in error.

9.3 Hybrid Key-Transport Methods

Key transport may be accomplished following any of the key-establishment schemes in this Recommendation (i.e, any **KAS1, KAS2** or **KTS-OAEP** scheme) by using an **approved** key-wrapping algorithm (see SP 800-38F[25]) with a key-wrapping key established during the execution of that key-establishment scheme. The security properties for this hybrid key-establishment process depend on the key-establishment scheme, the key-wrapping algorithm and the communication protocol used; the roles assumed by the participants during the process; and all other parameters used during the entire process.

---

[25] SP 800-38F, *Recommendation for Block Cipher Modes of Operation: Methods for Key Wrapping.*

10 Rationale for Selecting a Specific Scheme

The subsections that follow describe the security properties that may be considered when a user and/or developer is choosing a key-establishment scheme from among the various schemes described in this Recommendation. The descriptions are intended to highlight certain similarities and differences between families of key-establishment schemes and/or between schemes within a particular family; they do not constitute an in-depth analysis of all possible security properties of every scheme under all adversary models.

The (brief) discussions will focus on the extent to which each participant in a particular transaction has assurance that fresh keying material has been successfully established with the intended party (and no one else). To that end, it is important to distinguish between the actual identifier of a participant in a key-establishment transaction and the role (party U or party V) assumed by that participant during the transaction. To simplify matters, in what follows, assume that the actual identifiers of the (honest) participants in a key-establishment transaction are the proverbial "Alice," acting as party U, and "Bob," acting as party V. (Pretend, for the sake of discussion, that these identifiers are unique among the universe of possible participants.) The identifier associated with their malevolent adversary is "Eve." The discussions will also consider the ill effects of certain compromises that might occur. The basic security properties that are cited depend on such factors as how a shared secret is calculated, how keying material is established, and what types of key-confirmation (if any) are incorporated into a given scheme.

Note 1: In order to provide concise descriptions of security properties possessed by the various schemes, it is necessary to make some assumptions concerning the format and type of data that is used as input during key derivation. The following assumptions are made solely for the purposes of Sections 10.1 through 10.3; they are not intended to preclude the options specified elsewhere in this Recommendation.

1. When discussing the security properties of schemes, it is assumed that the *FixedInfo* input to a (single-step) key-derivation function employed during a particular key-agreement transaction uses either the concatenation format or the ASN.1 format (see Section 5.5). It is also assumed that *FixedInfo* includes sufficiently specific identifiers for the participants in the transaction, an identifier for the key-establishment scheme being used during the transaction, and additional input (e.g., a nonce, and/or session identifier) that may provide assurance to one or both participants that the derived keying material will reflect the specific context in which the transaction occurs (see Section 5.5 and Appendix B of SP 800-56A for further discussion concerning context-specific information that may be appropriate for inclusion in *FixedInfo*).

2. In general, *FixedInfo* may include additional secret information (already shared between parties U and V), but the following analyses of the security properties of each scheme type assume that additional secret information is not included in the *FixedInfo*.

3. In cases where an **approved** extraction-then-expansion key-derivation procedure is employed (see Section 5.5 and SP 800-56C), it is assumed that the *FixedInfo* is used as the *Context* input during the key-expansion step, as specified in SP 800-56C.

4. Finally, it is assumed that all required nonces employed during a transaction are random nonces that include a component consisting of a random bit string formed in accordance with the recommendations of Section 5.4.

Note 2: Different schemes may possess different security properties. A scheme should be selected based on how well the scheme fulfills system requirements. For instance, if messages are exchanged over a large-scale network where each exchange consumes a considerable amount of time, a scheme with fewer exchanges during a single key-agreement transaction might be preferable to a scheme with more exchanges, even though the latter may possess more security benefits. It is important to keep in mind that a key-establishment scheme is usually a component of a larger protocol that may offer security-related assurances beyond those that can be provided by the key-establishment scheme alone. For example, the protocol may include specific features that limit opportunities for accidental or intentional misuse of the key-establishment component of the protocol. Protocols, per se, are not specified in this Recommendation.

10.1 Rationale for Choosing a KAS1 Key-Agreement Scheme

In both schemes included in the **KAS1** family, only Bob (assumed to be acting as party V) is required to own an RSA key pair that is used in the key-agreement transaction. Assume that the identifier used to label party V during the transaction is one that is associated with Bob's RSA public key in a manner that is trusted by Alice (who is acting as party U). This can provide Alice with some level of assurance that she has correctly identified the party with whom she will be establishing keying material if the transaction is successfully completed.

Each **KAS1** scheme requires Alice to employ the RSASVE.GENERATE operation to select a (random) secret value Z and encrypt it as ciphertext C using Bob's RSA public key. Unless Bob's corresponding private key has been compromised, Alice has assurance that no unintended entity (i.e., no one but Bob) could employ the RSASVE.RECOVER operation to obtain Z from C. Absent the compromise of Bob's RSA private key and/or Z, Alice may attain a certain level of confidence that she has correctly identified party V as Bob. Alice's level of confidence is dependent upon:

- The specificity of the identifier that is associated with Bob's RSA public key,

- The degree of trust in the association between that identifier and the public key,

- The assurance of the validity of the public key, and

- The availability of evidence that the keying material has been correctly derived by Bob using Z (and the other information input to the agreed-upon key-derivation method), e.g., through key confirmation with Bob as the provider.

In general, Bob has no assurance that party U is Alice, since Bob has no assurance concerning the accuracy of any identifier that may be used to label party U (unless, for example, the protocol using a key-agreement scheme from the **KAS1** family also includes additional elements that establish a trusted association between an identifier for Alice and the ciphertext C that she contributes to the transaction while acting as party U).

The assurance of freshness of the derived keying material that can be obtained by a participant in a **KAS1** transaction is commensurate with the participant's assurance that different input will be supplied to the agreed-upon key-derivation method during each such transaction. Alice can obtain assurance that fresh keying material will be derived based on her unilateral selection and contribution of the random Z value. Bob can obtain similar assurance owing to his selection and contribution of the nonce N_V, which is also used as input to the agreed-upon key-derivation method.

The **KAS1-Party_V-confirmation** scheme permits party V to provide evidence to party U that keying material has been correctly derived. When the **KAS1-Party_V-confirmation** scheme is employed during a key-agreement transaction, party V provides a key-confirmation MAC tag, *MacTag_V*, to party U as specified in Section 8.2.3.2. This allows Alice (who is acting as party U, the key-confirmation recipient) to obtain assurance that party V has possession of the *MacKey* derived from the shared secret Z (and nonce N_V) and has used it with the appropriate *MacData_V* to compute the received *MacTag_V*. In the absence of a compromise of secret information (e.g., Bob's RSA private key and/or Z), Alice can also obtain assurance that the appropriate identifier has been used to label party V, and that the participant acting as party V is indeed Bob, the owner of the RSA public key associated with that identifier.

Specifically, by successfully comparing the received value of *MacTag_V* with her own computation, Alice (acting as party U, the key-confirmation recipient) may obtain assurance that

1. Party V has correctly recovered Z from C, and, therefore, possesses the RSA private key corresponding to Bob's RSA public key – from which it may be inferred that party V is Bob;

2. Both parties have correctly computed (at least) the same *MacKey* portion of the derived keying material;

3. Both parties agree on the values (and representation) of ID_V, ID_U, N_V, C, and any other data included in *MacData_V*; and

4. Bob (acting as party V) has actively participated in the transaction.

Consequently, when the **KAS1-Party_V-confirmation** scheme is employed during a particular key-agreement transaction (and neither Z nor Bob's RSA private key has been compromised), Alice can obtain assurance of the active (and successful) participation by Bob in the transaction.

The acquisition of Bob's RSA private key by their adversary, Eve, may lead to the compromise of shared secrets and derived keying material from past, current, and future legitimate transactions (i.e., transactions that involve honest parties and are not actively influenced by an adversary) that employ the compromised private key. For example, Eve may be able to compromise a particular **KAS1** transaction between Alice and Bob as long as she acquires the ciphertext, C, contributed by Alice and the nonce, N_V, contributed by Bob (as well as any other data used as input during key derivation). In addition to compromising legitimate **KAS1** transactions, once Eve has learned Bob's RSA private key, she may be able to impersonate Bob while acting as party V in future **KAS1** transactions (with Alice or any other party). Other schemes and applications that rely on the compromised private key may also be adversely affected. (See the appropriate subsection for details.)

Even without knowledge of Bob's private key, if Eve learns the value of Z that has been (or will be) used in a particular **KAS1** transaction between Alice and Bob, then she may be able to derive the keying material resulting from that transaction as easily as Alice and Bob (as long as Eve also acquires the value of N_V and any other data used as input during key derivation). Alternatively, armed with knowledge of the Z value that has been (or will be) selected by Alice, Eve might be able to insert herself into the transaction (in the role of party V) while masquerading as Bob.

10.2   Rationale for Choosing a KAS2 Key-Agreement Scheme

In the schemes included in the **KAS2** family, both Alice (assumed to be acting as party U) and Bob (assumed to be acting as party V) are required to own an RSA key pair that is used in their key-agreement transaction. Assume that the identifier used to label party V during the transaction is one that is associated with Bob's RSA public key in a manner that is trusted by Alice. Similarly, assume that the identifier used to label party U during the transaction is one that is associated with Alice's RSA public key in a manner that is trusted by Bob. This can provide each party with some level of assurance concerning the identifier of the other party, with whom keying material will be established if the transaction is successfully completed.

Each **KAS2** scheme requires Alice to employ the RSASVE.GENERATE operation to select a (random) secret value Z_U and encrypt it as ciphertext C_U using Bob's RSA public key. Unless Bob's corresponding private key has been compromised, Alice has assurance that no unintended entity (i.e., no one but Bob) could employ the RSASVE.RECOVER operation to obtain Z_U from C_U. Similarly, each **KAS2** scheme requires Bob to employ the RSASVE.GENERATE operation to select a (random) secret value Z_V and encrypt it as ciphertext C_V using Alice's RSA public key. Unless Alice's corresponding private key has been compromised, Bob has assurance that no unintended entity (i.e., no one but Alice) could employ the RSASVE.RECOVER operation to obtain Z_V from C_V.

Absent the compromise of Bob's RSA private key and/or Z_U, Alice may attain a certain level of confidence that she has correctly identified party V as Bob. Alice's level of confidence is commensurate with:

- The specificity of the identifier that is associated with Bob's RSA public key,

- The degree of trust in the association between that identifier and Bob's public key,

- The assurance of the validity of the public key, and

- The availability of evidence that the keying material has been correctly derived by Bob using $Z = Z_U \parallel Z_V$ (and the other information input to the agreed-upon key-derivation method), e.g., through key-confirmation, with Bob as the provider.

Similarly, absent the compromise of Alice's private key and/or Z_V, Bob may attain a certain level of confidence that he has correctly identified party U as Alice. Bob's level of confidence is commensurate with:

- The specificity of the identifier that is associated with Alice's RSA public key,

- The degree of trust in the association between that identifier and Alice's public key,

- The assurance of the validity of the public key, and

- The availability of evidence that the keying material has been correctly derived by Alice using $Z = Z_U \parallel Z_V$ (and the other information input to the agreed-upon key-derivation method), e.g., through key-confirmation, with Alice as the provider.

The assurance of freshness of the derived keying material that can be obtained by a participant in a **KAS2** transaction is commensurate with the participant's assurance that different input will be supplied to the agreed-upon key-derivation method during each such transaction. Alice can obtain assurance that fresh keying material will be derived, based on her selection and contribution of the random Z_U component of Z. Bob can obtain similar assurance owing to his selection and contribution of the random Z_V component of Z.

Evidence that keying material has been correctly derived may be provided by using one of the three schemes from the **KAS2** family that incorporates key confirmation. The **KAS2-Party_V-confirmation** scheme permits party V (Bob) to provide evidence of correct key derivation to party U (Alice); the **KAS2-Party_U-confirmation** scheme permits party U (Alice) to provide evidence of correct key derivation to party V (Bob); the **KAS2-bilateral-confirmation** scheme permits each party to provide evidence of correct key derivation to the other party.

When the **KAS2-Party_V-confirmation** scheme or the **KAS2-bilateral-confirmation** scheme is employed during a key-agreement transaction, party V provides a key-confirmation MAC tag, *MacTag$_V$*, to party U as specified in Section 8.3.3.2 or Section 8.3.3.4, respectively. This allows Alice (who is the recipient of *MacTag$_V$*) to obtain assurance that party V has possession of the *MacKey* derived from the shared secret Z and has used it with the appropriate *MacData$_V$* to compute the received *MacTag$_V$*. In the absence of a compromise of secret information (e.g., Bob's RSA private key and/or Z_U), Alice can also obtain assurance that the appropriate identifier has been used to label party V, and that the participant acting as party V is indeed Bob, the owner of the RSA public key associated with that identifier.

Similarly, when the **KAS2-Party_U-confirmation** scheme or the **KAS2-bilateral-confirmation** scheme is employed during a key-agreement transaction, party U provides a key-confirmation MAC tag, *MacTag$_U$*, to party V as specified in Section 8.3.3.3 or Section 8.3.3.4, respectively. This allows Bob (who is the recipient of *MacTag$_U$*) to obtain assurance that party U has possession of the *MacKey* derived from the shared secret Z and has used it with the appropriate *MacData$_U$* to compute the received *MacTag$_U$*. In the absence of a compromise of secret information (e.g., Alice's RSA private key and/or Z_V), Bob can also obtain assurance that the appropriate identifier has been used to label party U, and that the participant acting as party U is indeed Alice, the owner of the RSA public key associated with that identifier.

Specifically, by successfully comparing the value of a received MAC tag with his/her own computation, a key-confirmation recipient in a **KAS2** transaction (be it Alice or Bob) may obtain the following assurances.

1. He/She has correctly decrypted the ciphertext that was produced by the other party and, thus, that he/she possesses the RSA private key corresponding to the RSA public key that was used by the other party to produce that ciphertext – from which it may be inferred that the other party had access to the RSA public key owned by the key-confirmation recipient. For example, if Alice is a key-confirmation recipient, she may obtain assurance that she has correctly decrypted the ciphertext C_V using her RSA private key, and so may also obtain assurance that her corresponding RSA public key was used by party V to produce C_V.

2. The ciphertext sent to the other party was correctly decrypted and, thus, the other party possesses the RSA private key corresponding to the RSA public key that was used to

produce that ciphertext – from which it may be inferred that the other party is the owner of that RSA public key. For example, if Alice is a key-confirmation recipient, she can obtain assurance that party V has correctly decrypted the ciphertext C_U using the RSA private key corresponding to Bob's RSA public key – from which she may infer that party V is Bob.

3. Both parties have correctly computed (at least) the same *MacKey* portion of the derived keying material.

4. Both parties agree on the values (and representation) of ID_V, ID_U, C_V, C_U, and any other data included as input to the MAC algorithm.

5. Assuming that there has been no compromise of either participant's RSA private key and/or either component of Z, a key-confirmation recipient in a **KAS2** transaction can obtain assurance of the active (and successful) participation in that transaction by the owner of the RSA public key associated with the key-confirmation provider. For example, if Alice is a key-confirmation recipient, she can obtain assurance that Bob has actively – and successfully – participated in that **KAS2** transaction.

The acquisition of a single RSA private key by their adversary, Eve, will not (by itself) lead to the compromise of derived keying material from legitimate **KAS2** transactions between Alice and Bob that employ the compromised RSA key pair. (In this context, a "legitimate transaction" is one in which Alice and Bob act honestly, and there is no active influence exerted by Eve.) However, if Eve acquires an RSA private key, she may be able to impersonate that RSA key pair's owner while participating in **KAS2** transactions. (For example, If Eve acquires Alice's private key, she may be able to impersonate Alice – acting as party U or as party V – in **KAS2** transactions with Bob or any other party). Other schemes and applications that rely on the compromised private key may also be adversely affected. (See the appropriate subsection for details.)

Similarly, the acquisition of one (but not both) of the secret Z components, Z_U or Z_V, would not (by itself) compromise the keying material derived during a legitimate **KAS2** transaction between Alice and Bob in which the compromised value was used as one of the two components of Z. However, armed with knowledge of only one Z component, Eve could attempt to launch an active attack against the party that generated it. For example, if Eve learns the value of Z_U that has been (or will be) contributed by Alice, then Eve might be able to insert herself into the transaction by masquerading as Bob (while acting as party V). Likewise, an adversary who knows the value of Z_V that has been (or will be) selected by Bob might be able to participate in the transaction by masquerading as Alice (while acting as party U).

10.3 Rationale for Choosing a KTS-OAEP Key-Transport Scheme

In each of the key-transport schemes included in the **KTS-OAEP** family, only Bob (assumed to be acting as party V, the key-transport receiver) is required to own an RSA key pair that is used in the transaction. Assume that the identifier used to label party V during the transaction is one that is associated with Bob's RSA public key in a manner that is trusted by Alice (who is acting as party U, the key-transport sender). This can provide Alice with some level of assurance that she has correctly identified the party with whom she will be establishing keying material if the key-transport transaction is successfully completed.

99

Each **KTS-OAEP** scheme requires Alice to employ the RSA-OAEP.ENCRYPT operation to encrypt the selected keying material (and any additional input) as ciphertext C, using Bob's RSA public key. Unless Bob's corresponding private key has been compromised, Alice has assurance that no unintended entity (i.e., no one but Bob) could employ the RSA-OAEP.DECRYPT operation to obtain the transported keying material from C. Absent the compromise of Bob's RSA private key (or some compromise of the keying material itself – perhaps prior to transport), Alice may attain a certain level of confidence that she has correctly identified party V as Bob. Alice's level of confidence is commensurate with:

- The specificity of the identifier that is associated with Bob's RSA public key,

- The degree of trust in the association between that identifier and the public key,

- The assurance of the validity of the public key, and

- The availability of evidence that the transported keying material has been correctly recovered from C by Bob, e.g., through key confirmation, with Bob as the provider.

In general, Bob has no assurance that party U is Alice, since Bob has no assurance concerning the accuracy of any identifier that may be used to label party U (unless, for example, the protocol using a key-transport scheme from the **KTS-OAEP** family also includes additional elements that establish a trusted association between an identifier for Alice and the ciphertext, C, that she sends to Bob while acting as party U).

Due to Alice's unilateral selection of the keying material, only she can obtain assurance of its freshness. (Her level of confidence concerning its freshness is dependent upon the actual manner in which the keying material is generated by/for her.) Given that Bob simply accepts the keying material that is transported to him by Alice, he has no assurance that it is fresh.

The randomized plaintext encoding used during the RSA-OAEP.ENCRYPT operation can provide assurance to Alice that the value of C will change from one **KTS-OAEP** transaction with Bob to the next, which may help obfuscate the occurrence of a repeated transport of the same keying material from Alice to Bob, should that ever be necessary.

The **KTS-OAEP-Party_V-confirmation** scheme permits party V to provide evidence to party U that keying material has been correctly recovered from the ciphertext C. When the **KTS-OAEP-Party_V-confirmation** scheme is employed during a key-transport transaction, party V provides a key-confirmation MAC tag ($MacTag_V$) to party U as specified in Section 9.2.4.2. This allows Alice (who is acting as party U, the key-confirmation recipient) to obtain assurance that party V has recovered the fresh MAC key ($MacKey$) that was included in the transported keying material and that party V has used it with the appropriate $MacData_V$ to compute the received $MacTag_V$. In the absence of a compromise of secret information (e.g., Bob's RSA private key and/or the MAC key), Alice can also obtain assurance that the appropriate identifier has been used to label party V, and that the participant acting as party V is indeed Bob, the owner of the RSA public key associated with that identifier.

Specifically, by successfully comparing the received value of $MacTag_V$ with her own computation, Alice (acting as party U, the key-confirmation recipient) may obtain assurance that

1. Party V has correctly recovered *MacKey* from *C*, and, therefore, possesses the RSA private key corresponding to Bob's RSA public key – from which it may be inferred that party V is Bob;

2. Both parties agree on the values (and representation) of ID_V, ID_U, *C*, and any other data included in *MacData$_V$*; and

3. Bob has actively participated in the transaction (as party V), assuming that neither the transported MAC key nor Bob's RSA private key has been compromised. Alice's level of confidence is commensurate with her confidence in the freshness of the MAC key.

The acquisition of Bob's RSA private key by their adversary, Eve, may lead to the compromise of keying material established during past, current, and future legitimate transactions (i.e., transactions that involve honest parties and are not actively influenced by an adversary) that employ the compromised private key. For example, Eve may be able to compromise a particular **KTS-OAEP** transaction between Alice and Bob, as long as she also acquires the ciphertext, *C*, sent from Alice to Bob. In addition to compromising legitimate **KTS-OAEP** transactions, once Eve has learned Bob's RSA private key, she may be able to impersonate Bob while acting as party V in future **KTS-OAEP** transactions (with Alice or any other party). Other schemes and applications that rely on the compromised private key may also be adversely affected. (See the discussions of other schemes in this section.)

Even without knowledge of Bob's private key, if the **KTS-OAEP-Party_V-confirmation** scheme is used during a particular key-transport transaction, and Eve learns the value of *MacKey* that Alice will send to Bob, then it may be possible for Eve to mislead Alice about Bob's (active and successful) participation. As long as Eve also acquires the value of *C* intended for Bob (and any other data needed to form *MacData$_V$*), it may be possible for Eve to correctly compute *MacTag$_V$* and return it to Alice as if it had come from Bob (who may not even be aware that Alice has initiated a transaction with him). Such circumstances could arise, for example, if (in violation of this Recommendation) Alice were to use the same MAC key while attempting to transport keying material to multiple parties (including both Bob and Eve).

10.4　Summary of Assurances Associated with Key-Establishment Schemes

The security-related features discussed in the preceding subsections of Section 10 can be summarized in terms of the following types of assurance that may be obtained when participating in a key-establishment transaction.

- **Implicit Key Authentication (IKA)**: In the case of a key-agreement scheme from the **KAS1** or **KAS2** family, this is the assurance obtained by one party in a key-agreement transaction that only a specifically identified entity (the intended second party in that transaction) could also derive the key(s) of interest. In the case of a key-transport scheme from the **KTS-OAEP** family, this is the assurance obtained by the sender that only a specifically identified entity (the intended receiver in that transaction) could successfully decrypt the encrypted keying material to obtain the key(s) of interest.

- **Key Freshness (KF)**: This is the assurance obtained by one party in a key-establishment transaction that keying material established during that transaction is statistically independent of the keying material established during that party's previous key-establishment transactions.

- **Key Confirmation (KC)**: This is the assurance obtained by one party in a key-establishment transaction that a specifically identified entity (the intended second party in that key-establishment transaction) has correctly acquired and is able to use, the key(s) of interest.

Notes:

A participant in a key-establishment transaction cannot hope to distinguish between the actions of another entity and the actions of those who share knowledge of that entity's private key-establishment key and/or any other secret data sufficient for that entity's successful participation in a particular key-agreement transaction. In what follows, references to a "specifically identified entity" must be interpreted as an umbrella term including all those who are legitimately in possession of that entity's private key, etc., and are trusted to act on the entity's behalf. Any assurance obtained with respect to the actions of a specifically identified entity is conditioned upon the assumption that the identified entity's relevant private/secret data has not been misused by a trusted party or compromised by an adversary.

IKA assurance, as used in this Recommendation, does not address the potential compromise of established keying material owing to such problems as improper storage, the failure to prevent the leakage of sensitive information during computations involving the established keys, and/or inadequate methods for the timely destruction of sensitive data (including the keys themselves). These are just a few examples of misuse, mishandling, side-channel leakage, etc. that could lead to an eventual compromise.

In the definition of KC assurance, this Recommendation's requirement that it be a specifically identified entity who demonstrates the ability to use (some portion of) the established keying material is a stricter condition than is sometimes found in the literature. In this Recommendation, KC assurance presupposes IKA assurance with respect to (at least) the MAC key used in the key-confirmation computations.

KC assurance can be obtained by employing a key-establishment scheme that includes key-confirmation as specified in this Recommendation. In particular, the KC provider is expected to use an RSA private key, and the KC recipient is expected to contribute random/ephemeral data that affects the values of both the *MacKey* and the *MacData* used to compute a key-confirmation *MacTag*.

The following table shows which types of assurance can be obtained and by whom (i.e., party U and/or party V) in a key-establishment transaction by using appropriately implemented schemes from the indicated scheme families. The previous assumptions in Section 10 concerning the format and content of *FixedInfo*, the specificity of identifiers bound to RSA public keys, the randomness of nonces, etc., still hold.

Table 3: Summary of Assurances.

Scheme Family	Sections	Assurance that can be Obtained by the Indicated Parties		
		IKA	KF	KC
KAS1	8.2 and 10.1	U	U & V	U
KAS2	8.3 and 10.2	U & V	U & V	U & V
KTS-OAEP	9.2 and 10.3	U	U	U

In key-agreement transactions that employ a scheme from the **KAS2** family, there is an additional type of assurance that can be obtained by both participants:

- **Key-Compromise Impersonation Resilience (K-CI)**: This is the assurance obtained by one party in a **KAS2** key-agreement transaction that the compromise of that party's RSA private key would not permit an adversary to impersonate another entity (the owner of a second, uncompromised, RSA key pair) while acting as the second party in the transaction.

  For example, suppose that Alice participates in a **KAS2** key-agreement transaction with a second party that she believes to be Bob (based on the identifier associated with the second party's RSA public key). Alice has assurance that even if a malicious party, Eve, has obtained Alice's RSA private key, that would not (by itself) permit Eve to impersonate Bob in the transaction and successfully establish shared keying material with Alice.

The notion of key-compromise impersonation resilience, as defined in this Recommendation, is not applicable to transactions employing a scheme from the **KAS1** or **KTS-OAEP** family. In such schemes, only one party owns an RSA key pair, and the scheme (by itself) provides no means of ensuring the accuracy of any identifier that may be associated with the other party.

Under the assumptions made in Section 10, there is an often-desirable type of assurance that is not supported by the use of (only) the key-establishment schemes specified in this Recommendation:

- **Forward Secrecy (FS)**: This is the assurance obtained by one party in a key-establishment transaction that the keying material established during that transaction is secure against the future compromise of (any and all of) the long-term private/secret keys of the participants.

(Key-agreement transactions that employ a scheme from the **KAS2** family afford some security against the compromise of a single participant's RSA private key, but may not be secure against the compromise of the RSA private keys of both participants.) If a user or application requires assurance of forward secrecy, then an appropriate choice of key-agreement scheme from the C(2) category of schemes specified in SP 800-56A may be employed.

11 Key Recovery

For some applications, the secret keying material used to protect data or to process protected data may need to be recovered (for example, if the normal reference copy of the secret keying material is lost or corrupted). In this case, either the secret keying material or sufficient information to reconstruct the secret keying material needs to be available (for example, the keys and other inputs to the scheme used to perform the key-establishment process).

When a key-recover capability is required, the handling/management of keys and other information used during the key-establishment process **shall** require long-term storage of the following data, as needed, to facilitate recovery of established keying material:

1. One or both keys of a key pair and/or.

2. A key-wrapping key.

In addition, the following information that is used during key-establishment may need to be saved:

3. The nonce(s),

4. The ciphertext,

5. Additional input, and

6. *OtherInput*, or its equivalent.

General guidance on key recovery and the protections required for each type of key is provided in SP 800-57.

12   Implementation Validation

When the NIST Automatic Cryptographic Validation Protocol (ACVP) has extended its testing capabilities with this Recommendation, a vendor **shall** have its implementation tested and validated by the Cryptographic Algorithm Validation Program (CAVP) and Cryptographic Module Validation Program (CMVP) in order to claim conformance to this Recommendation. Information on the CAVP and CMVP is available at https://csrc.nist.gov/projects/cryptographic-algorithm-validation-program and https://csrc.nist.gov/projects/cryptographic-module-validation-program, respectively.

An implementation claiming conformance to this Recommendation **shall** include one or more of the following capabilities:

- Key-pair generation as specified in Section 6.3, together with an **approved** random bit generator;

- Public-key validation as specified in Section 6.4.2;

- A key-agreement scheme from Section 8, together with an **approved** key-derivation method from Section 5.5 and an **approved** random bit generator;

- The key-transport scheme specified in Section 9.2, together with an **approved** random bit generator and **approved** hash function(s); and/or

- Unilateral or bilateral key confirmation as specified in Section 5.6.

An implementer **shall** also identify the appropriate specifics of the implementation, including:

- The hash function(s) to be used (see Section 5.1);

- The MAC function used for key confirmation;

- The *MacKey* length(s) (see Table 1 in Section 5.6.3);

- The key-establishment schemes available (see Sections 8 and 9);

- The key-derivation method to be used if a key-agreement scheme is implemented, including the format of *OtherInput* or its equivalent (see Section 5.5);

- The type of nonces to be generated (see Section 5.4);

- How assurance of private-key possession and assurance of public-key validity are expected to be achieved by both the owner and the recipient (see Section 6.4);

- Whether or not a capability is available to handle additional input (see Section 9.1); and

- The RBG used, and its security strength (see Section 5.3).

Appendix A: References

A.1 Normative References

[ANS X9.44]   Accredited Standards Committee X9 (2007) *Public Key Cryptography for the Financial Services Industry: Key Establishment Using Integer Factorization Cryptography*. (American National Standards Institute), American National Standard for Financial Services (ANS) X9.44-2007 (R2017), August 2007, 2017 release, Withdrawn.

[FIPS 140]   National Institute of Standards and Technology (2002) *Security Requirements for Cryptographic Modules*. (U.S. Department of Commerce, Washington, D.C.), Federal Information Processing Standards Publication (FIPS) 140-2, May 25, 2001 (Change Notice 2, 12/3/2002). https://doi.org/10.6028/NIST.FIPS.140-2

[FIPS 140 IG]   National Institute of Stanards and Technology, Canadian Centre for Cyber Security (2003) *Implementation Guidance for FIPS 140-2 and the Cryptographic Module Validation Program*, [Amended]. Available at https://csrc.nist.gov/csrc/media/projects/cryptographic-module-validation-program/documents/fips140-2/fips1402ig.pdf.

[FIPS 180]   National Institute of Standards and Technology (2015) *Secure Hash Standard (SHS)*. (U.S. Department of Commerce, Washington, D.C.), Federal Information Processing Standards Publication (FIPS) 180-4, August 2015. https://doi.org/10.6028/NIST.FIPS.180-4

[FIPS 186]   National Institute of Standards and Technology (2013) *Digital Signature Standard (DSS)*. (U.S. Department of Commerce, Washington, D.C.), Federal Information Processing Standards Publication (FIPS) 186-4, July 2013. https://doi.org/10.6028/NIST.FIPS.186-4

[FIPS 197]   National Institute of Standards and Technology (2001) *Advanced Encryption Standard (AES)*. (U.S. Department of Commerce, Washington, D.C.), Federal Information Processing Standards Publication (FIPS) 197, November 2001. https://doi.org/10.6028/NIST.FIPS.197

[FIPS 198]   National Institute of Standards and Technology (2008) *The Keyed-Hash Message Authentication Code (HMAC)*. (U.S. Department of Commerce, Washington, D.C.), Federal Information Processing Standards Publication (FIPS) 198-1, July 2008. https://doi.org/10.6028/NIST.FIPS.198-1

[FIPS 202]   National Institute of Standards and Technology (2015) *SHA-3 Standard: Permutation-Based Hash and Extendable-Output Functions*. (U.S. Department of Commerce, Washington, D.C.), Federal Information Processing Standards Publication (FIPS) 202, August 2015. https://doi.org/10.6028/NIST.FIPS.202

[ISO/IEC 8825] International Organization for Standardization/International Electrotechnical Commission (2015) *ISO/IEC 8825-1:2015 – Information Technology – ASN.1 encoding rules: Specification of Basic Encoding Rules (BER), Canonical Encoding*

Rules (CER) and Distinguished Encoding Rules (DER) (International Organization for Standardization, Geneva, Switzerland), 5th Ed.

[PKCS 1]   Moriarty K (ed.), Kaliski B, Jonsson J, Rush A (2016) *PKCS #1: RSA Cryptography Specifications Version 2.2.* (Internet Engineering Task Force), IETF Request for Comments (RFC) 8017. https://doi.org/10.17487/RFC8017

[SP 800-38B]   Dworkin MJ (2016) *Recommendation for Block Cipher Modes of Operation: the CMAC Mode for Authentication.* (National Institute of Standards and Technology, Gaithersburg, Maryland), NIST Special Publication (SP) 800-38B, May 2005 (includes updates as of 10/06/2016). https://doi.org/10.6028/NIST.SP.800-38B

[SP 800-38C]   Dworkin MJ (2007) *Recommendation for Block Cipher Modes of Operation: the CCM Mode for Authentication and Confidentiality.* (National Institute of Standards and Technology, Gaithersburg, Maryland), NIST Special Publication (SP) 800-38C, May 2004 (includes updates as of 07/20/2007). https://doi.org/10.6028/NIST.SP.800-38C

[SP 800-38F]   Dworkin MJ (2012) *Recommendation for Block Cipher Modes of Operation: Methods for Key Wrapping.* (National Institute of Standards and Technology, Gaithersburg, Maryland), NIST Special Publication (SP) 800-38F, December 2012. https://doi.org/10.6028/NIST.SP.800-38F

[SP 800-56A]   Barker EB, Chen L, Roginsky A, Vassilev A, Davis R (2018) *Recommendation for Pair-Wise Key-Establishment Schemes Using Discrete Logarithm Cryptography.* (National Institute of Standards and Technology, Gaithersburg, Maryland), NIST Special Publication (SP) 800-56A, Rev. 3, April 2018. https://doi.org/10.6028/NIST.SP.800-56Ar3

[SP 800-56C]   Barker EB, Chen L, Davis R (2018) *Recommendation for Key-Derivation Methods in Key-Establishment Schemes.* (National Institute of Standards and Technology, Gaithersburg, Maryland), NIST Special Publication (SP) 800-56C, Rev. 1, April 2018. https://doi.org/10.6028/NIST.SP.800-56Cr1

[SP 800-57]   Barker EB (2016) *Recommendation for Key Management, Part 1: General.* (National Institute of Standards and Technology, Gaithersburg, Maryland), NIST Special Publication (SP) 800-57 Part 1, Rev. 4, January 2016. https://doi.org/10.6028/NIST.SP.800-57pt1r4

[SP 800-89]   Barker EB (2006) *Recommendation for Obtaining Assurances for Digital Signature Applications.* (National Institute of Standards and Technology, Gaithersburg, Maryland), NIST Special Publication (SP) 800-89, November 2006. https://doi.org/10.6028/NIST.SP.800-89

[SP 800-90]   Recommendation for Random Number Generation

Barker EB, Kelsey JM (2015) *Recommendation for Random Number Generation Using Deterministic Random Bit Generators.* (National Institute of Standards and

Technology, Gaithersburg, Maryland), NIST Special Publication (SP) 800-90A, Rev. 1, June 2015. https://doi.org/10.6028/NIST.SP.800-90Ar1

Sönmez Turan M, Barker EB, Kelsey JM, McKay KA, Baish M, Boyle M (2018) *Recommendation for the Entropy Sources Used for Random Bit Generation.* (National Institute of Standards and Technology, Gaithersburg, Maryland), NIST Special Publication (SP) 800-90B, January 2018. https://doi.org/10.6028/NIST.SP.800-90B

Barker EB, Kelsey JM (2016) *Recommendation for Random Bit Generator (RBG) Constructions.* (National Institute of Standards and Technology, Gaithersburg, Maryland), Draft (2nd) NIST Special Publication (SP) 800-90B, April 2016. Available at: https://csrc.nist.gov/publications/detail/sp/800-90c/draft

[SP 800-108]   Chen L (2008) *Recommendation for Key Derivation Using Pseudorandom Functions (Revised).* (National Institute of Standards and Technology, Gaithersburg, Maryland), NIST Special Publication (SP) 800-108, October 2009. https://doi.org/10.6028/NIST.SP.800-108

[SP 800-133]   Barker EB, Roginsky A (2012) *Recommendation for Cryptographic Key Generation.* (National Institute of Standards and Technology, Gaithersburg, Maryland), NIST Special Publication (SP) 800-133, December 2012. https://doi.org/10.6028/NIST.SP.800-133

[SP 800-135]   Dang QH (2015) *Recommendation for Existing Application-Specific Key Derivation Functions.* (National Institute of Standards and Technology, Gaithersburg, Maryland), NIST Special Publication (SP) 800-135, Rev. 1, December 2011. https://doi.org/10.6028/NIST.SP.800-135r1

[SP 800-185]   Kelsey JM, Chang S-jH, Perlner RA (2016) *SHA-3 Derived Functions: cSHAKE, KMAC, TupleHash, and ParallelHash.* (National Institute of Standards and Technology, Gaithersburg, Maryland), NIST Special Publication (SP) 800-185, December 2016. https://doi.org/10.6028/NIST.SP.800-185

A.2 Informative References

[Boneh 1999]   Boneh D (1999) Twenty Years of Attacks on the RSA Cryptosystem. *Notices of the American Mathematical Society* 46(2):203-213. Available at https://www.ams.org/notices/199902/boneh.pdf

[HN 1998]   Håstad J, Näslund M (1998) The Security of Individual RSA Bits. *Proceedings of the 39th Annual Symposium on Foundations of Computer Science (FOCS),* (IEEE Computer Society, Palo Alto, California), pp. 1-10. https://doi.org/10.1109/SFCS.1998.743502

[Manger 2001]   Manger J (2001) A Chosen Ciphertext Attack on RSA Optimal Asymmetric Encryption Padding (OAEP) as Standardized in PKCS #1 v2.0. *Advances in Cryptology – Crypto 2001* (Springer, Berlin), pp. 230-238. https://doi.org/10.1007/3-540-44647-8_14

[RSA 1978]   Rivest RL, Shamir A, Adleman L (1978) A Method for Obtaining Digital Signatures and Public-Key Cryptosystems. *Communications of the ACM* 21(2):120-126. https://doi.org/10.1145/359340.359342

Appendix B: Data Conversions (Normative)

B.1 Integer-to-Byte String (I2BS) Conversion

Input: A non-negative integer X and the intended length n of the byte string satisfying $2^{8n} > X$.

Output: A byte string S of length n bytes.

1. $Q_{n+1} = X$.

2. For $i = n$ to 1 by -1

    2.1 $Q_i = \lfloor (Q_{i+1})/256 \rfloor$.

    2.2 $X_i = Q_{i+1} - (Q_i \times 256)$.

    2.3 $S_i = (a_{i1}, a_{i2}, a_{i3}, a_{i4}, a_{i5}, a_{i6}, a_{i7}, a_{i8})$,

        the 8-bit binary representation of the non-negative integer
        $X_i = a_{i1}2^7 + a_{i2}2^6 + a_{i3}2^5 + a_{i4}2^4 + a_{i5}2^3 + a_{i6}2^2 + a_{i7}2 + a_{i8}$.

3. Let $S_1, S_2, ..., S_n$ be the bytes of S from leftmost to rightmost.

4. Output S.

B.2 Byte String to Integer (BS2I) Conversion

Input: A non-empty byte string S (*SLen* is used to denote the length of the byte string).

Output: A non-negative integer X.

1. Let $S_1, S_2, ... S_{SLen}$ be the bytes of S from first to last (i.e., from leftmost to rightmost).

2. Let $X = 0$.

3. For $i = 1$ to *SLen* by 1

    3.1 Let $X_i = (a_{i1}2^7 + a_{i2}2^6 + a_{i3}2^5 + a_{i4}2^4 + a_{i5}2^3 + a_{i6}2^2 + a_{i7}2 + a_{i8})$,
            where $a_{i1}, a_{i2}, a_{i3}, a_{i4}, a_{i5}, a_{i6}, a_{i7}, a_{i8}$ are the bits of S_i from leftmost to rightmost;
            i.e., $S_i = (a_{i1}, a_{i2}, a_{i3}, a_{i4}, a_{i5}, a_{i6}, a_{i7}, a_{i8})$.

    3.2 Replace X by $(X \times 256) + X_i$.

4. Output X.

Appendix C: Prime-Factor Recovery (Normative)

Two methods for prime-factor recovery are provided below: Appendix C.1 provides a probabilistic method, and Appendix C.2 provides a determinitic method. Prime-factor recovery is required during key-pair validation using the basic format (see Section 6.4.1.2.1).

C.1 Probabilistic Prime-Factor Recovery

The following algorithm recovers the prime factors of a modulus, given the public and private exponents. The algorithm is based on Fact 1 in [Boneh 1999].

Function call: RecoverPrimeFactors(n, e, d)

Input:

1. n: modulus.

2. e: public exponent.

3. d: private exponent.

Output:
1. (p, q): prime factors of modulus.

Errors: "prime factors not found"

Assumptions: The modulus n is the product of two prime factors p and q; the public and private exponents satisfy $de \equiv 1 \pmod{\lambda(n)}$ where $\lambda(n) = \text{LCM}(p - 1, q - 1)$.

Process:

1. Let $m = de - 1$. If m is odd, then go to Step 4.

2. Write m as $m = 2^t r$, where r is the largest odd integer dividing m, and $t \geq 1$.

3. For $i = 1$ to 100 do:

    a. Generate a random integer g in the range $[0, n{-}1]$.

    b. Let $y = g^r \bmod n$.

    c. If $y = 1$ or $y = n - 1$, then go to Step g.

    d. For $j = 1$ to $t - 1$ do:

        i.   Let $x = y^2 \bmod n$.

        ii.   If $x = 1$, go to Step 5.

        iii. If $x = n - 1$, go to Step g.

        iv. Let $y = x$.

    e. Let $x = y^2 \bmod n$.

    f. If $x = 1$, go to Step 5.

    g. Continue.

4. Output "prime factors not found," and exit without further processing.

5. Let $p = \text{GCD}(y - 1, n)$ and let $q = n/p$.

6. Output (p, q) as the prime factors.

Any local copies of $d, p, q, m, t, r, x, y, g$ and any intermediate values used during the execution of the RecoverPrimeFactors function **shall** be destroyed prior to or during steps 4 and 6. Note that this includes the values for p and q that are output in step 6.

Notes:

1. According to Fact 1 in [Boneh 1999], the probability that one of the values of y in an iteration of Step 3 reveals the factors of the modulus is at least 1/2, so on average, no more than two iterations of that step will be required. If the prime factors are not revealed after 100 iterations, then the probability is overwhelming that the modulus is not the product of two prime factors, or that the public and private exponents are not consistent with each other.

2. The algorithm bears some resemblance to the Miller-Rabin primality-testing algorithm (see, e.g., FIPS 186).

3. The order of the recovered prime factors p and q may be the reverse of the order in which the factors were generated originally.

4. All local copies of d, p, q, and and any other local/intermediate values used during the execution of the RecoverPrimeFactors function **shall** be destroyed prior to the early termination of the process due to an error, or (in the absence of errors), prior to or during the the completion of step 6.

C.2 Deterministic Prime-Factor Recovery

The following (deterministic) algorithm also recovers the prime factors of a modulus, given the public and private exponents. A proof of correctness is provided below.

Function call: RecoverPrimeFactors(n, e, d)

Input:

1. n: modulus.

2. e: public exponent.

3. d: private exponent.

Output:

    (p, q): prime factors of modulus, with $p > q$.

Assumptions:

1. The modulus n is the product of two prime factors p and q, with $p > q$.

2. Both p and q are less than $2^{(nBits/2)}$, where $nBits \geq 2048$ is the bit length of n.

3. The public exponent e is an odd integer between 2^{16} and 2^{256}.

4. The private exponent d is a positive integer that is less than $\lambda(n) = \mathrm{LCM}(p - 1, q - 1)$.

5. The exponents e and d satisfy $de \equiv 1 \pmod{\lambda(n)}$.

Note: For more general applications of the process below, assumptions 2 and 3 above can be replaced by the more general assumption that the public exponent e is an odd integer satisfying $1 < e^2 \leq n/(p + q - 1)$. (See the discussion following Lemma 3 below.) That condition will be satisfied, e.g., if e^2 is greater than one, but no greater than one-half of the smallest prime factor of n, as is the case for any RSA key pair generated in conformance with this Recommendation.

Process:

1. Let $a = (de - 1) \times \mathrm{GCD}(n - 1, de - 1)$.

2. Let $m = \lfloor a/n \rfloor$ and $r = a - mn$, so that

    $$a = mn + r \quad \text{and} \quad 0 \leq r < n.$$

3. Let $b = ((n - r)/(m + 1)) + 1$; if b is not an integer or $b^2 \leq 4n$, then output an error indicator, and exit without further processing. (See Note 1 below.)

4. Let Y be the positive square root of $b^2 - 4n$; if Y is not an integer, then output an error indicator, and exit without further processing. (See Note 2 below.)

5. Let $p = (b + Y)/2$ and let $q = (b - Y)/2$.

6. Output (p, q) as the prime factors. (See Note 3 below.)

Notes:

1. b should be equal to $p + q$. If b is not an integer satisfying $b^2 > 4n$, then one or more of the assumptions concerning n, e, d, p and q are incorrect and the corresponding RSA key pair does not conform to the requirements of this Recommendation.

2. Y should be equal to $p - q$. If Y is not an integer, then one or more of the assumptions concerning n, e, d, p and q are incorrect and the corresponding RSA key pair does not conform to the requirements of this Recommendation.

3. The labeling of the recovered prime factors (i.e., labeling the larger as p and the smaller as q) may be the reverse of the labeling that was used when those factors were originally generated.

4. All local copies of d, p, q, and and any other local/intermediate values used during the execution of the RecoverPrimeFactors function **shall** be destroyed prior to the early

termination of the process due to an error, or (in the absence of errors) prior to or during the the completion of step 6.

Proof of Correctness:

Since (by definition), $\lambda(n) = \text{LCM}(p - 1, q - 1)$,

$$(p - 1)(q - 1) = \text{LCM}(p - 1, q - 1) \times \text{GCD}(p - 1, q - 1) = \lambda(n) \times \text{GCD}(p - 1, q - 1) \qquad (1)$$

Lemma 1: $\text{GCD}(p - 1, q - 1) = \text{GCD}(n - 1, \lambda(n))$

Proof of Lemma 1:

Since $n - 1 = (p - 1)(q - 1) + (p - 1) + (q - 1)$ and $\lambda(n)$ is a divisor of $(p - 1)(q - 1)$, it follows that $\text{GCD}(n - 1, \lambda(n)) = \text{GCD}((p - 1) + (q - 1), \lambda(n))$.

Any common divisor of $p - 1$ and $q - 1$ will also be a divisor of both $(p - 1) + (q - 1)$ and $\lambda(n)$, and hence a divisor of $\text{GCD}((p - 1) + (q - 1), \lambda(n))$. In particular, $\text{GCD}(p - 1, q - 1)$ is a divisor of $\text{GCD}((p - 1) + (q - 1), \lambda(n))$, and so, $\text{GCD}(p - 1, q - 1) \leq \text{GCD}((p - 1) + (q - 1), \lambda(n))$.

To establish that $\text{GCD}((p - 1) + (q - 1), \lambda(n)) \leq \text{GCD}(p - 1, q - 1)$ – and hence that the two GCDs are equal. Let $\{ h_i \mid 1 \leq i \leq m \}$ denote the set of primes that are divisors of either $p - 1$ or $q - 1$. Then the factorizations of $p - 1$, $q - 1$, and $\lambda(n)$ have the forms

$$p - 1 = h_1^{x(1)} \times h_2^{x(2)} \times \ldots \times h_m^{x(m)},$$

$$q - 1 = h_1^{y(1)} \times h_2^{y(2)} \times \ldots \times h_m^{y(m)}, \text{ and}$$

$$\lambda(n) = h_1^{z(1)} \times h_2^{z(2)} \times \ldots \times h_m^{z(m)},$$

where $\{ x(i) \mid 1 \leq i \leq m \}$, $\{ y(i) \mid 1 \leq i \leq m \}$, and $\{ z(i) \mid 1 \leq i \leq m \}$ are sets of non-negative integers satisfying $z(i) = \max(x(i), y(i))$. If j is a divisor of $\lambda(n)$, then j has the form

$$j = h_1^{w(1)} \times h_2^{w(2)} \times \ldots \times h_m^{w(m)}, \text{ with } 0 \leq w(i) \leq z(i) \text{ for } 1 \leq i \leq m.$$

Suppose that j is also a divisor of $(p - 1) + (q - 1)$ and that, for a particular value of i, $z(i) = x(i)$. In this case, $h_i^{w(i)}$ will divide both $p - 1$ and the sum $(p - 1) + (q - 1)$, hence $h_i^{w(i)}$ will divide their difference, $q - 1$. Similarly, if $z(i) = y(i)$, then $h_i^{w(i)}$ will divide both $q - 1$ and the sum $(p - 1) + (q - 1)$, hence $h_i^{w(i)}$ will divide $p - 1$ as well. Thus, each prime-power factor of j is a common divisor of $p - 1$ and $q - 1$, and so the same is true of j. This shows that any common divisor j of $\lambda(n)$ and the sum $(p - 1) + (q - 1)$ is also a common divisor of $p - 1$ and $q - 1$, and hence a divisor of $\text{GCD}(p - 1, q - 1)$.

In particular, $\text{GCD}((p - 1) + (q - 1), \lambda(n))$ is a divisor of $\text{GCD}(p - 1, q - 1)$, from which it follows that $\text{GCD}((p - 1) + (q - 1), \lambda(n)) \leq \text{GCD}(p - 1, q - 1)$. Combining this result with the previously established inequality $\text{GCD}(p - 1, q - 1) \leq \text{GCD}((p - 1) + (q - 1), \lambda(n))$, proves the lemma's claim: $\text{GCD}(p - 1, q - 1) = \text{GCD}((p - 1) + (q - 1), \lambda(n)) = \text{GCD}(n - 1, \lambda(n))$.

Combining Lemma 1 with equation (1) above yields

$$(p - 1)(q - 1) = \lambda(n) \times \text{GCD}(n - 1, \lambda(n)). \tag{2}$$

Consider the quantity $a = (de - 1) \times \text{GCD}(n, de - 1)$ from step 1 of the RecoverPrimeFactors process. Since $e > 1$, the congruence $de \equiv 1 \pmod{\lambda(n)}$ implies that $de - 1 = u\lambda(n)$ for some positive integer u. Substituting $u\lambda(n)$ for $de - 1$ in the expression for a yields

$$a = (de - 1) \times \text{GCD}(n - 1, de - 1) = u\lambda(n) \times \text{GCD}(n - 1, u\lambda(n)). \tag{3}$$

$\text{GCD}(n - 1, \lambda(n))$ is a common divisor of $n - 1$ and $u\lambda(n)$, and so is also a divisor of their GCD. Let $v = \text{GCD}(n - 1, u\lambda(n)) / \text{GCD}(n - 1, \lambda(n))$.

Lemma 2: $1 \le v \le u < e$

Proof of Lemma 2:

The assumption that the positive integer d is less than $\lambda(n)$ and the fact that $u = (de - 1)/\lambda(n)$ implies that $u < e$. Since v is a positive integer, it is true that $1 \le v$. It remains to show that $v \le u$. Using

$$\text{GCD}(n - 1, u\lambda(n)) = (n - 1)(u\lambda(n)) / \text{LCM}(n - 1, u\lambda(n))$$

and

$$\text{GCD}(n - 1, \lambda(n)) = (n - 1)(\lambda(n)) / \text{LCM}(n - 1, \lambda(n)),$$

It follows that

$$v = \text{GCD}(n - 1, u\lambda(n)) / \text{GCD}(n - 1, \lambda(n)) = u \times \text{LCM}(n - 1, \lambda(n))/\text{LCM}(n - 1, u\lambda(n)),$$

which can be rewritten to obtain

$$\text{LCM}(n - 1, u\lambda(n)) / \text{LCM}(n - 1, \lambda(n)) = u/v.$$

Since $\text{LCM}(n - 1, u\lambda(n))$ is a common multiple of $n - 1$ and $\lambda(n)$, it is a multiple of the least common multiple of $n - 1$ and $\lambda(n)$. Therefore, $u/v = \text{LCM}(n - 1, u\lambda(n))/\text{LCM}(n - 1, \lambda(n))$ is a positive integer. From $1 \le u/v$, one obtains $v \le u$, completing the proof of the lemma.

Using $\text{GCD}(n - 1, u\lambda(n)) = v\text{GCD}(n - 1, \lambda(n))$ together with equations (2) and (3) above, it follows that

$$a = u\lambda(n) \times v\text{GCD}(n - 1, \lambda(n)) = uv(\lambda(n) \times \text{GCD}(n - 1, \lambda(n))) = uv(p - 1)(q - 1). \tag{4}$$

Since $(p - 1)(q - 1) = n - (p + q - 1)$, equation (4) above shows that

$$a = uvn - uv(p + q - 1) = (uv - 1)n + (n - uv(p + q - 1)) \tag{5}$$

Lemma 3: $0 \le n - uv(p + q - 1) < n$

Proof of Lemma 3:

It suffices to verify that $0 < uv \le n/(p + q - 1)$. By the assumptions on the sizes of p, q, and n, it follows that $p + q - 1 < 2^{(nBits/2)+1}$ and $n > 2^{(nBits - 1)}$, so that $n/(p + q - 1) > 2^{(nBits/2) - 2}$. If it can be shown that the product uv is less than $2^{(nBits/2) - 2}$, then the proof of Lemma 3 will be complete. Lemma 2 implies that $1 \le uv \le u^2 < e^2$. By assumption, $e < 2^{256}$, so $e^2 < 2^{512}$. Since this document requires $nBits \ge 2048$, it follows that $2^{(nBits/2) - 2} \ge 2^{1022}$. The fact that $uv < 2^{512} < 2^{1022} \le 2^{(nBits/2) - 2}$ completes the proof of the lemma.

Note: Lemma 3 (and hence the proof of correctness for the RecoverPrimeFactors process) is true under conditions more general than those used in the proof above, which invoked the bounds on the sizes of e, p, q, and n that are required by this Recommendation. For example, it suffices to know that those four values satisfy the condition $1 < e^2 \le n/(p + q - 1)$ and that $d < \lambda(n)$.

Now consider the quantities m and r computed in step 2 of the RecoverPrimeFactors process. Combining equation (5) with Lemma 3 yields

$$m = \lfloor a/n \rfloor = (uv - 1) \quad \text{and} \quad r = a - mn = n - uv(p + q - 1).$$

Therefore, in step 3 of the process,

$$b = (\,(n - r)/(m + 1)\,) + 1 = (\,uv(p + q - 1))/(uv)\,) + 1 = p + q,$$

and in step 4,

$$\Upsilon = (b^2 - 4n)^{1/2} = (\,(p + q)^2 - 4pq)^{1/2} = (\,(p - q)^2)^{1/2} = p - q.$$

These values for b and Υ ensure that p and q are correctly recovered in step 5, since

$$p = (b + \Upsilon)/2 \quad \text{and} \quad q = (b - \Upsilon)/2.$$

Appendix D: Maximum Security Strength Estimates for IFC Modulus Lengths

Approved key-establishment schemes are required to provide a security strength of at least 112 bits. An approximation of the maximum security strength that can be supported by an RSA modulus n can be computed as follows:

Let $nBits = \text{len}(n)$, the bit length of the RSA modulus n included in a public key employed by the key-establishment scheme. The estimated maximum security strength E that can be supported by the modulus is determined using the following formula:

$$E = \frac{1.923 \times \sqrt[3]{(nBits \times \ln 2)} \times \sqrt[3]{[\ln(nBits \times \ln 2)]^2} - 4.69}{\ln 2} \quad .$$

Since E is not likely to be an integer, some rounding is appropriate. To facilitate comparison to symmetric-key algorithms (whose keys typically consist of some number of bytes), the value of E will be rounded to the nearest integer multiple of eight to obtain an estimate of the maximum security strength that can be supported by the use of a modulus of length $nBits$. In short,

$$\text{ES}(nBits) = \text{the nearest multiple of 8 to } E.$$

Therefore, for the modulus lengths identified in Table 2 of Section 6.3, the maximum security strengths that can be supported are provided below.

Table 4: Estimated Security Strengths of Common RSA Moduli

Modulus Length (in bits)	E	Maximum Security Strength ES(*nBits*)
2048	110.1	112
3072	131.97	128
4096	149.73	152
6144	178.42	176
8192	201.7	200

As stated in Section 6.3, any modulus with an even bit length that provides at least 112 bits of security strength may be used (i.e., *nBits* must be an even integer ≥ 2048). The method above can be used to estimate the security strengths supported by moduli other than those explicitly listed above.

Appendix E: Revisions (Informative)

In the 2014 revision, the following revisions were made:

- Section 3.1 – Added definitions of assumptions, binding, destroy, fresh, key-derivation function, key-derivation method, key-wrapping key, MAC tag, and trusted association; removed algorithm identifier, digital signature, initiator, responder.

- Section 4 – Used party U and party V to name the parties, rather than using the initiator and responder as the parties. In Sections 8 and 9, the schemes have been accordingly renamed: KAS1-responder-confirmation is now KAS1-Party_V-confirmation, KAS2-responder-confirmation is now KAS2-Party_V-confirmation, KAS2-initiator-confirmation is now KAS2-Party_U-confirmation, KTS-OAEP-receiver-confirmation is not KTS-OAEP-Party_V-confirmation, and KTS-KEM-KWS-receiver-confirmation is now KTS-KEM-KWS-Party_V-confirmation.

- Section 4 – Added requirements to destroy the local copies of secret and private values and all intermediate calculations before terminating a routine normally or in response to an error. Instructions to this effect have been inserted throughout the document.

- The discussion about identifiers vs. identity and binding have been moved to Section 4.1.

- Section 4.3 – The phrase "IFC-based" has been removed throughout the document.

- Section 5.4 – More discussion has been added about the use of nonces, including new requirements and recommendations.

- Section 5.5 – Key derivation has been divided into single-step key derivation methods (Section 5.5.1), an extract-then-expand key derivation procedure (Section 5.5.2) and application-specific key-derivation methods (Section 5.5.3).

- Section 5.5.1.2 – The use of *OtherInfo* (including identifiers) during the derivation of keys is recommended, but no longer required (Section 5.5.1.2).

- Moved the general introduction of key-confirmation to Section 5.9 – The discussion now incorporates the material from Section 6.6 of the previous version of the document.

- Section 6.4 – There is now a longer, and more thorough discussion of validity in Section 6.4. The concept of trusted associations has been introduced.

- Section 6.4.1.1 – Removed "or TTP" from the following: "The key pair can be revalidated at any time by the owner as follows…."

- Section 7.2.3.2 – Moved discussion of symmetric key-wrapping methods from Section 5.7 to Section 7.2.3.2; much more information is now provided.

- Section 10 – The rationale for choosing each scheme type has been combined in this new section, along with a discussion of their security properties.

- The old Appendix A, Summary of Differences between this Recommendation and ANS X9.44 (Informative), was removed.

- The old Appendix E becomes Appendix D, and the changes introduced in this Revision are listed here.

- All figures are replaced to reflect the content, text, and terminology changes.

- Security requirements have been updated; in particular, the 80-bit security strength is no longer permitted in this Recommendation.

- Changes to handle the destruction of local keys and intermediate values have been introduced.

- General changes have been made to make this Recommendation more similar to [SP 800 56A].

In the 2018 revision, the following changes were made (in addition to editorial changes):

1. Overall changes:

   - Removed provisions for using TDEA.

   - Provided moduli > 3072 bits and a method for estimated the maximum security strength that can be provided by these moduli.

   - Removed the KTS-KEM-KWS scheme and added a hybrid scheme (KTS-Hybrid-SKW).

   - Hyperlinks to sections within the document and to referenced documents are now included.

2. Section 3.1: Added: *Big endian, Byte length, Confidentiality, Key-establishment key pair, Integrity, Random nonce, Support (a security strength), Symmetric key.*

   - Modified: *Approved, Assurance of validity, Bit length, Byte, Destroy, Fresh,* Identifier, *Key-agreement transaction, Key confirmation, Key-derivation function, Key-derivation method, Key-derivation procedure, Key establishment, Key-establishment transaction, Keying material, Key transport, Key-transport transaction, Key wrapping,* Key-wrapping key, *Least-common multiple, MacOutputBits, MacOutputLen, MAC tag, MacTagBits, Message Authentication Code, Nonce, Party, Public-key certificate, Recipient, Scheme, Security properties, Targeted security strength, Trusted third party.*

   - Deleted: *Entity authentication, Length in bits of the non-negative integer x .*

3. Section 3.2: Added: *len(x)*, which has been used throughout the document; ES*(nBits); MacKeyBits; MacOutputBits; MacOutputLen; MacTagBits; OtherInput.*

   - Modified: *c; C, C$_0$, C$_1$; nLen;*
   - Removed: *Bytelen, k, KTS-KEM-KWS, kwkBits, KWS, OtherInfo, RSA-KEM-KWS, RSA-KEM-KWS-basic, RSA-KEM-KWS-PartyV-confirmation, x, z.*

4. Section 4.1, para. 2: A sentence was inserted to provide guidance for providing a key pair to its owner.

5. Section 4.2, para. 1: A sentence was inserted as sentence 3 (for clarification).

6. Section 4.3: Discussion about the the RSA-KEM-KWS scheme has been removed. A reference to the hybrid method for key transport has been inserted. Figure 3 was modified.

7. Section 5.2: The first three paragraphs were updated. KMAC was added as an approved MAC algorithm.

8. Section 5.4, third para.: Reworded the requirements for the minimum security strength and random bit string length for a nonce.

9. Section 5.5: Rewritten to refer to SP 800-56C for performing key derivation.

10. Section 5.6: Inserted text and a table to clarify the roles for each scheme.

11. Sections 5.6.1 and 5.6.2: Revised to accommodate the new **KTS-Hybrid SKW** family of schemes.

12. Section 5.6.3: Revised to clarify the approved MAC algorithms, the acceptable *MacKey* lengths and the supported security strengths.

13. Section 6.2.1: Steps 3a and 3b have been rewritten.

14. Section 6.3: Inserted text and a table of estimated maximum security strengths for additional approved modulus lengths. Also, see Appendix D.

15. Sections 6.3.1.1, 6.3.2.1, and 6.4.1.2.1: Revised to accommodate the revised modulus lengths and clarify error indications.

16. Sections 6.4.1.2.1, 6.4.1.2.2, 6.4.1.2.3, 6.4.1.3.2, 6.4.1.3.3, 6.4.1.4.2 and 6.4.1.4.3: Added step 3c to check that *nBits* is an even integer.

17. Section 6.4.1.2.1: Added a requirement regarding the error rate on the primality tests.

18. Section 6.4.1.5: Revised step 2 to clarify KAS2 key confirmation.

19. Section 6.4.2.3.2: Revised descriptions of the key confirmation provided for the key-establishment schemes.

20. Old Section 7: Removed the components used by the KTS-KEM-KWS family of schemes.

21. Section 7.1.2: Routines have been added for decryption using the prime factor and CRT formats for the private key.

22. Section 7.2.2.1: Explicitly stated that the hash function used for the MGF computation need not be the same as the has function used for MAC generation.

23. Section 7.2.2, 7.2.2.3 and 7.2.2.4: Removed the list of (limited) modulus lengths that were used in the previous version of SP 800-56B.

24. Section 7.2.2.4: Added an initial step to set *DecryptErrorFlag* to *False*,

25. Section 8.2.3.2: Added a sentence to the first paragraph about key confirmation providing assurance to party U.

26. Section 8.3, item 6: Provided further information about unilateral and bilateral key confirmation.

27. Section 8.3.3.2: Added a sentence to the first paragraph about key confirmation providing assurance to party U.

28. Section 8.3.3.3: Added a sentence to the first paragraph about key confirmation providing assurance to party V.

29. Section 8.3.3.4: Added a sentence to the first paragraph about key confirmation providing assurance to both parties.

30. Section 9: Revised to remove discussions of the KTS-KEM-KWS schemes and a brief discussion of a hybrid key-transport scheme.

31. Section 9.1: Revised to refer to the list in Section 5.5.2 as possible information to be used for additional input.

32. Section 9.2.4.2: Added a sentence to the first paragraph about key confirmation providing assurance to party U.

33. Section 9.3: A discussion of a hybrid key-transport method.

34. Section 10.4: Removed the rationale for the RSA-KEM KWS family and added a summary of the assurances for each key-establishment scheme family.

35. Section 12: Additional items were added to the validation lists.

36. Appendix A: Updated the references.

37. Appendix B.2: Step 3.1 has been rewritten.

38. Appendix C.2: Added the Deterministic Prime-Factor Recovery Method.

39. Appendix D: Added a method for estimated the maximum security strength that could be provided by an IFC modulus length.

www.ingramcontent.com/pod-product-compliance
Lightning Source LLC
Chambersburg PA
CBHW060152060326
40690CB00018B/4078